BURIED

BURIED

KEN WYLIE

UPDATED EDITION

RMB

This book is dedicated to the families and friends who lost the following loved ones at La Traviata on January 20, 2003, in the Selkirk Mountains of British Columbia:

Dave Finnerty
Naomi Heffler
Craig Kelly
Kathy Kessler
Ralph (Vern) Lunsford
Jean-Luc Schwendener
Dennis Yates

Updated Edition

For information on purchasing bulk quantities of this book, or to obtain media excerpts or invite the author to speak at an event, please visit rmbooks.com and select the "Contact" tab.

RMB | Rocky Mountain Books Ltd.
rmbooks.com
@rmbooks
facebook.com/rmbooks

Cataloguing data available from Library and Archives Canada
ISBN 9781771603850 (paperback)
ISBN 9781771603867 (electronic)

Cover photo: BC Coroner Crown Fracture Measurement, La Traviata Avalanche site, January 21, 2003

Printed and bound in Canada

We would like to also take this opportunity to acknowledge the traditional territories upon which we live and work. In Calgary, Alberta, we acknowledge the Niitsítapi (Blackfoot) and the people of the Treaty 7 region in Southern Alberta, which includes the Siksika, the Piikuni, the Kainai, the Tsuut'ina and the Stoney Nakoda First Nations, including Chiniki, Bearpaw, and Wesley First Nations. The City of Calgary is also home to Métis Nation of Alberta, Region III. In Victoria, British Columbia, we acknowledge the traditional territories of the Lkwungen (Esquimalt, and Songhees), Malahat, Pacheedaht, Scia'new, T'Sou-ke and W̱SÁNEĆ (Pauquachin, Tsartlip, Tsawout, Tseycum) peoples.

We acknowledge the financial support of the Government of Canada through the Canada Book Fund and the Canada Council for the Arts, and of the province of British Columbia through the British Columbia Arts Council and the Book Publishing Tax Credit.

Canada

Canada Council for the Arts | Conseil des arts du Canada

British Columbia | British Columbia Arts Council
An agency of the Province of British Columbia

CONTENTS

ACKNOWLEDGEMENTS

Several people deserve special mention because they were stewards of the book the entire way. My mother, Sylvia, was skeptical about the project at the start, but grew in her support, perspective and belief, which in the end was priceless. Barbara Michelsen housed us for many months during several stages of the writing and provided great conversations and exchanges of ideas. Mark Miller's friendship, honest feedback and ability to listen helped me focus on what was important through the process of living in the work. My sisters, Shauna Gill and Debbie Mayer, were there for me in supporting the book, and our relationship has grown in ways that are immeasurable because of it. And finally, Keith Haberl understood this journey without me having to explain anything.

I would also and especially like to thank the following family members of the avalanche victims: Howard Heffler, Brian Kelly, Gillian Kelly, Scott Kessler, Lizbeth Kranabitter, Corinna Laemmerzahl, Peter Millar, Annie Polucha, Carol Schneider-Yates and Janet Witzler. All of you had the courage to connect with me in person, by email or over the telephone. Each of you respected the story I had to tell without judgment and with compassion. I value the lessons each of you taught me. All of you contributed more than I can say to this book. Bless all of you for your generosity and forgiveness.

Many people have also helped me to write this book by reading the manuscript, giving me their feedback verbally or in writing, and supporting a multitude of aspects of this project. These people are this book's community and are presented here in alphabetical order: Lindsay Andersen, Leanne Allison, Frank Baumann (RIP), Nicholas Beer, William Björndahl, Lynn Bowering, John Buffery, Mike Burgess, Myrl Coulter, Gwen Curry, Jamie Cowan, Danielle Daniel, Tony Daffern, Mary Ellen Donnan, Bruce Elkin, Paddy Gerome, Charles Goodsell, Curtis Green, Scott Gullion, Diny Harrison, Karsten Heuer, Jan Redford, Charlotte Hughes, Scott Kennedy, Jayson Krause, Giovanna Longhi, Warren MacDonald, Eric Malone, Dennis McDade, Megan Michelson, Mark Miller, Lynn Moorman, Jeff Nazarchuk, Julian Norris, Joe Pavelka, Randy Richards, Laura Robinson, Beth Rutter, Anne Ryall, Rivanne Sandler, Chic Scott, Marilyn Simonds, Lena Soots, Brian Spear, Rochelle Squires, Larry Stanier, Steve Swenson, Margo Talbot, Dharini Woolcombe, Sharon Wood and Daryl Wylie.

I am also grateful for the efforts of the many people who experienced the avalanche and other events described in this book and shared their stories with me. Their recollections, notes and letters made a huge difference in the final manuscript by jogging my memory with large and small events: Heidi Biber, Charles Bieler, Jeff Bullock, Eduardo Figueroa, Diny Harrison, Jeff Nazarchuk, Eric Malone, Joe Pojar, Rick Reynolds, John Siebert and Bruce Stewart. I would also like to thank those who assisted me in researching the event: Hugh Finlay, Bruce Jameson, Paul Maloney, Chico Newell (B.C. coroner), Dave Stark, the late Randy Starkman, Larry Stanier and Ilya Storm.

The anchors of this book are the belief, courage and vision of publisher Don Gorman and his team at Rocky Mountain Books. This book took courage to edit, print and stand behind, and Don has been like a rock through the entire process. I am also grateful to Karl Siegler, the editor who kept demanding both more and less from me and had the brilliance to know how to draw out what was in me the whole time. And to Chyla Cardinal, who made it all look good.

AUTHOR'S NOTE

This book is my best effort to convey what remains in my heart about the La Traviata avalanche tragedy of January 20, 2003.

In a few instances, the perfect chronology of the story has been modified to convey the best possible picture of all of the characters in this narrative. But every detail of these stories has been carefully researched from my notes and from countless email conversations I've had with those who were present at the events described.

Drafts of the included "lesson stories" were sent to friends with whom I experienced them. This work is now as accurate as I am able to make it.

However, in researching the technical details about La Traviata – things like the exact weather conditions and snowfall amounts – I was denied access to the official records of Selkirk Mountain Experience. I compensated for this gap by gathering information from the Baumann and Stanier reports cited in the References section and from the Environment Canada weather records for nearby Mt. Fidelity.

The views expressed in this book are my own and do not reflect those of the publishing company, its staff or its affiliates.

On a final note, these pages constitute the thread composing the larger tapestry of the whole life I have lived to date, of which La Traviata has become the centre. My ultimate aim is to take responsibility for my actions and learn from their consequences.

CHAPTER 1

THE DURRAND GLACIER

JANUARY 18, 2003

The pilot deftly lands the yellow, orange, red and blue helicopter on the level pad to the east of the chalet cradled by the Selkirk Mountains that soar to the heights in all directions. The inverted mushroom cloud of snow whirled up by the main rotor disperses as the helicopter's motor winds down to a high-pitched idle. Formidable glaciers tumble down the steep valleys of the surrounding craggy, snowy peaks.

The Selkirks offer all the key ingredients for backcountry skiing: exciting terrain, remoteness, abundance of snow and temperatures cold enough to make most of the snow that does fall light and fluffy. They arguably constitute the best mountain range on Earth to ski. Backcountry skiers call this "Tiger Country." Not for the faint of heart, the combination of steep slopes, deep snow and dramatic glaciation makes ski touring here serious business.

The chalet is a quaint brown wooden structure with

red shutters and "Swiss gingerbread" accents. It sits on a knoll at 6,360 feet, in the subalpine above Cairns Creek, out of reach of avalanches. In the summer it is surrounded by beautiful alpine meadows and small groves of stunted subalpine fir trees. Its massive wraparound wooden deck, now shovelled clear of snow, provides a place for guests to gaze upon spectacular peaks like Tumbledown Mountain, Mount Ruth and Diamond Peak, and the Cairns Creek valley far below.

The guests that come here intend to ski between five and six thousand human-powered vertical feet per day, all of it gained on the way up by using stick-on synthetic seal skins that allow one to ascend the peaks before skiing down them in a single run. During a typical week, a group will ski between 35 and 50 thousand vertical feet climbed one stride at a time, the enormous effort of the ascent enriching each exhilarating turn on the way down.

With my hat, ski goggles and ear protectors on, I open the helicopter doors on the left side. Using non-verbal commands in the deafening noise, I point the new guests to the snowy trail that leads to the chalet. With my other gloved hand in the stop position, I communicate to the overzealous outgoing guests to wait in the safe zone away from the rotating blades. Then I move to the helicopter's tail boom compartment, open the door and unload the incoming packs and duffle bags. Once done, I load the orange-flagged outgoing luggage, careful to get a good fit so that the cargo hold is filled to capacity, and close and secure the door. Now Ruedi Beglinger walks over with the outgoing guests that we skied with all last week and coaches them into the machine. With a slow, deliberate pace, I walk around the nose of the aircraft to the right side and unload incoming skis and snowboards from the long white ski basket mounted on the machine's right-hand skid, keeping them horizontal so they do not hit the main rotor. In the same careful way, I then load the orange-flagged outgoing skis. With the ski basket refilled, I close it with the two red-handled latches, double-checking them for security. Next, I crouch down on the right side of the machine beside the pilot, whom I now recognize as Paul Maloney. Ruedi makes a visual check with me and I see him give Paul the thumbs-up. The engine gains speed and momentum. With the rhythmic thump of the rotor blades, the helicopter becomes seemingly weightless, lifts off the ground, clears the outhouse, and then uses the steep drop-off down the Cairns Creek valley to gain speed and additional lift.

When all is quiet again, Ruedi walks towards me on the helipad and in a sharp Swiss accent says, "Ken! You have to be sure to get as much luggage in as you can with each flight! We can't afford to do an extra baggage run!"

His harsh words touch off a lifelong trigger inside me. I feel myself shrivel and crawl into a cave, where I glower and muster a deflated "Okay."

Ruedi, the owner of Selkirk Mountain Experience (SME), is slightly shorter than my five feet, ten inches, has piercing blue eyes, sandy brown hair with a bald patch on top and a craggy face that has seen decades of high-altitude sun. Intense energy maniacally fuels him, and although he is assertive, I notice that his eyes look up at me from a head tilted down. He projects a mastery of these mountains and is widely respected for his guiding skills.

Although it is only the start of my third week of work here at SME this season, I have come to expect Ruedi to lose his temper and go on a tirade at seemingly nothing on a regular basis. I find this side of his personality incredibly stressful. It makes me feel unsure about everything I do for fear it might elicit one of his rampages. This sets off a deep insecurity inside me. Though I sense my reaction to his tirades is wrong and know that it is often inappropriate, I feel powerless in the wake of these emotions. He turns on his heel and leaves me outside to bring the new guests' gear in.

I grab some of the bags piled on the helipad and haul them to the chalet. Some of the newly arrived guests meet me on the narrow snow path to get their luggage, where I greet them by shaking their gloved hands, noticing that they are both fit and eager, as usual. One of the new guests is Craig Kelly. Having guided him at Island Lake Lodge and because of the anticipatory talk Ruedi had given us before Craig's arrival, I know him as a world-champion snowboarder who is now working on becoming a ski guide. He is warm and gracious as he shakes my hand and we reacquaint. He joins me in my work hauling bags and I appreciate the effort.

Once we deposit the remaining outgoing bags in the lodge, I return to the quiet helipad and think, *It shouldn't be long for the next flight. It's a short trip to staging.* In my mind's eye, I picture the gravel parking lot along the Big Bend Highway, about 14 kilometres north of Revelstoke.

A garbled message meets my ear from the SME radio, its scrambling program left on inadvertently. When people from outside the tour operation radio the chalet, the scramble function should be off on the SME radios so that we can hear the person trying to reach us. When the scramble function is on, there is no possibility of communication with outside radios. Open communication is important for switch-over days, or any other time communication with the outside world is required. I asked Ruedi when I started work here why there was a scrambler on our SME radios and he said, "So those people at Tangiers can't hear what's going on up here. What happens here is none of their business!" This radio protocol seems strange to me – a little paranoid, if truth were told.

I repeat the process of unloading and loading the next helicopter, and when the second-last flight leaves, my wife, Nancy, comes over wearing her yellow pack, organized and ready to leave. She has been up here cooking for us for the past week – it's been a rare occurrence in my 20-year outdoor guiding career to have Nancy to talk to in the evening. Usually I'd have been alone or with other guides at night while working. During our evening tête-à-têtes I have increasingly shared my unease about working here, and we continue these conversations on the helipad while waiting for the last group to arrive.

"Well, Nance, have a good time down in Revy," I say, trying to say goodbye on a positive note.

"Yes, I will," she says as she perks up. "Number one on my list is to do some tile work this week on the house. It's so amazing that we'll be moving in to our new home in just a few weeks."

"Yeah, I'm excited too. It'll be cool to live in the space we created together. It's also great that I'll get the time off to move."

"You be safe up here. It was scary seeing you guys ski the Goat Face the other day," she says, a note of concern re-entering her voice.

"I was a little nervous up there in the big terrain myself, but it's all about committing to the guests. I know a guide cannot make the right call 100 per cent of the time, so after the Goat Face, I asked Ruedi if he too had been nervous. He responded, 'When I make a call it's 100 per cent.' I'm not sure if he means he trusts his decisions 100 per cent once he has made them, or if he thinks he can't be wrong. He might be that good; I just don't know. I have this chronic uneasy feeling up here, and I'm not sure whether it's caused by Ruedi's intimidating character or by my fear of the hazards. When I'm around Ruedi, I just get all flustered and confused."

Nancy looks at me as if to say, "Perhaps it's both," but before she can articulate it, we hear the last helicopter coming and our focus shifts to servicing the flight. I make final adjustments to the outgoing baggage, put ear protectors and goggles on and hold down the lighter items on the waiting pile of gear. With another gale-force blast of air, the helicopter lands and we unload and then reload it with people and equipment.

Nancy gets in last, but before she climbs aboard, I give her a hug below the spinning rotors. Then I help her get into the rear seat of the machine, checking her and the guests' seat belts and carefully securing the doors. Crouching down in view of Paul, I give him a thumb's up, and they lift off. I notice the call letters C-GSML on the machine's lower nose as the craft lifts above me in a hover, then tilts forward to accelerate out of view. Within moments I feel the contrasting silence of the powerful alpine winter landscape and suddenly feel small and insignificant. I raise my head and pan my eyes across the snow-laden peaks partially shrouded by clouds. A deep loneliness rushes in to fill the void this quiet germinates.

The snow squeaks under my winter boots like milk powder squeezed in its plastic bag as I walk alone to the chalet. The thought *I'm not good enough to work here* inexplicably wells up in me again. I try to get a grip on my unease as I walk into the chalet, taking a deep breath to ground myself, and the dread dissipates for a moment as the smell of fresh baking wafts over from the kitchen. Inside, the guests are settling in, preparing for Ruedi's orientation talk on the workings of the place. The room is bright, with light streaming through the windows. The wood floor, pine panelling, cabinets and Swiss-style chairs give the place a warm golden glow. Most folks have already put together a lunch for themselves from the buffet laid out on the table closest to the front door. On the surface, it all seems so idyllic; I wish it were for me. There is a vague, unfocused fear that pervades everything for me here – I can neither put my finger on its cause, nor shake it. I feel powerless, like I did as a child. I find a chair and sit down along with everyone else, panning the room and wishing I had my notebook in hand to help me remember the names of this week's group. With a guest list I go over the names of people, matching them with the ones I met outside. Perusing my list I read:

Heidi Biber	Truckee, Calif.
Charles Bieler	New York City.
Jeff Birkiner	Calgary.
Paula Couturier	Revelstoke.
Dan Di Maria	Aspen.
Dave Finnerty	New Westminster.
Age Fluitman	The Netherlands.
Robyn Goodson	Seattle.
Naomi Heffler	Calgary.
Craig Kelly	Nelson.

Kathy Kessler	Truckee.
Keith Lindsay	Truckee.
Vern Lunsford	Littleton, Colorado.
Rick Martin	Truckee.
Joe Pojar	Staff
Rick Reynolds	Truckee.
Bruce Stewart	Truckee.
Jean-Luc Schwendener	Canmore.
John Siebert	Wasilla, Alaska.
Evan Weselake	Calgary.
Dennis Yates	Hollywood, Calif.

I also notice Paula, Jeff and Joe, all staff people here to ski this week.

Now Ruedi stands to address the group. In his thick, lilting Swiss accent, he says, "Welcome to da Durrand Glacier Chalet. I built dis place in nineteen eighty-fife. Each year I ski over a million vertical feet, guiding guests on some of the best skiing anywhere. We get over four metres of settled snow here at the chalet typically in a winter. We have been running ski tours up here every winter for the past 18 years and we have never had a serious accident in all of that time. However, what we are doing has hazards, and this morning you all signed a waiver down at the Wintergreen Inn. That means that you understand those risks. The fee that you have paid covers guiding, meals and accommodation. It does not cover helicopter fees charged if you hurt yourself and need to be airlifted out of here. If you want to buy additional insurance, come and speak with us. Now some staff introductions: my wife, Nicoline, is running the chalet; Kim is the cook and she produces wonderful meals for all of us to enjoy. The kitchen is off limits to guests; there is no reason for you to go in there. Kim is very busy and we do not want to get in her way. Ken is the assistant guide. He will ski with the slower group in behind me. Now a little bit about the chalet."

He goes over, in meticulous detail, exactly how he wants the guests to use the space. Then he paints a picture of the daily routine. "Breakfast each day is at 7:00 a.m. sharp. Before breakfast you can make your lunch and have it ready for the day. At the end of breakfast I will give you a briefing so you know where we are going, what mountain we will be skiing. Here we ski to the summits. If you want to go yo-yo skiing, you will have to go to one of the other lodges. The days keep moving because we come here to ski. There is not much time for hanging around out there. If you want to hang around, you can stay back here at the chalet.

"When you get home from skiing, there will be tea and baked goodies here in the chalet, you will have some time for a sauna, then dinner will be served at 7:00 p.m. Each morning everyone needs to be ready to ski exactly at 8:00 a.m. In a few minutes, I will assign you all an avalanche transceiver. You will wear the transceiver under some layers of clothing while skiing so that it doesn't get ripped off of you in an avalanche. Today you can wear them under your shell layer so they are close for practice. You need to know the number of your unit. Each day when you get home, make sure that you turn your transceiver off and hang it on the numbered hook by the back door. Don't take them to your rooms. Ken will be checking the units each evening to make sure that they're all switched off and we are not wasting batteries. Are there any questions?"

There is silence before he begins again, "In a moment, we will head down to the 'soccer field,' the big flat area south of the chalet, and go through the Avalanche Beacon School. You can get ready."

After the talk, there is a hurried energy in the group to get out the door, a mix of excitement and stress; nobody wants to be the last to be ready. In the entryway of the chalet, I slide my silver and red plastic ski boots on and step outside. It is overcast and snowing lightly with temperatures just below freezing. I position myself and my equipment on the southern end of the preparation area, step into my skis and switch my avalanche transceiver to the CH (Check) test mode. As the guests ski past me, I listen to my transceiver to hear if their units are broadcasting. In moments, most of the clients and Ruedi have left on the track leading south to the soccer field. Age Fluitman struggles with his snowboard skins right next to the chalet. He is tall and fair-skinned and speaks English with a Dutch accent. Nicoline helped me this morning with the pronunciation of his name. When I said "Age," she had corrected me, saying, "It's AAAHHUU, Ken," in a guttural tone. Now he seems visibly stressed, so I slide over to assist him. With my own internal clock ticking as I wonder if I will catch hell for being late at the soccer field, we work together to strenuously pull his very wide stick-on skins apart so that we can adhere them to his splitboard. Craig walks up, leaning his split snowboard against the ski rack, asking, "Can I help?"

"These fat skins are nearly impossible to get apart. The glue is so gummy. I think we nearly have them, though. But Age's bindings need a looking at as well," I say.

Craig is dark-haired, thin-faced, unshaven and has a lanky build, but his scruffy appearance is offset by his relaxed confidence, which puts both of us at ease.

Craig says, "Go on and catch up with Ruedi. We'll be right behind you."

I check that Age's and Craig's transceivers are transmitting and ski toward the soccer field, looking over my shoulder as I leave, second-guessing myself, wondering if I am doing the right thing. Sliding below the west-facing slope that leads to the group ahead, my mind replays the conversation Dave and Ruedi had had regarding Craig just yesterday.

Dave had said, "Hey, Ruedi, I hear that Craig Kelly is coming this next week. He's one of my snowboarding gurus."

Ruedi had replied: "Champion snowboarder – I will show him a thing or two about ski touring. He's coming because my snowboard sponsor, Burton, requested a week for him."

My own thoughts gather about Craig. I remember him from my 1998 season ski guiding at Island Lake Lodge, a snowcat-skiing operation near Fernie, British Columbia, where he is a shareholder. At the time, I had no clue about the snowboarding world. He was Craig the shareholder, easygoing and a gentle person. He would ride his snowboard down the line that I set, perfectly relaxed and happy with wherever we went. There had been only one time when he wanted to ride a slightly different line. He had asked me first, we checked it out, and he had laid beautiful, supple turns down the mountain. I am not surprised that he has chosen to hang back and happy he is willing to help Age out.

I stride along on my skis and enter the wide-open flat area that is the soccer field. I see Ruedi circled up with John, Keith and Rick, telling stories and having a good time; the others mingle in their own small groups. When I reach him he asks, "Is that everyone?"

"No. Craig is back with Age. Age was having trouble getting his brand-new skins apart and onto his splitboard. Craig is helping him."

"Okay," Ruedi says and turns back to telling stories.

A few stressful minutes pass. I keep glancing back at the slope coming down from the chalet and eventually see Craig and Age on the track to the soccer field.

Everyone gathers for Ruedi to begin the Avalanche Beacon School. He starts by assembling the group to the south of him. He pulls out a red Barryvox avalanche transceiver, and reviews all of the functions with the guests – on, off, battery test, transmit – then pushes the "mode" button three times to switch from transmitting a signal to receiving a signal. Each individual switches modes, producing all kinds of shrill beeping as the units pick up transmitting signals. Once everyone is on receive (and no unit is transmitting), there is silence again. He explains about the three search phases in an avalanche rescue: "There is the primary or signal search, the secondary search, where one follows the signal to the buried person from roughly 20 metres to within two metres, and then the pinpoint search, which brackets the victim down to a two-metre square."

Ruedi describes the transition from the secondary search to the pinpoint search as being like the airport approach of an airplane, where it moves more slowly and deliberately as well as dropping closer to the surface of the snow. He says, "The beacon has to be on the surface of the snow to home in on the strongest signal. Once you have that point, an avalanche probe is used to confirm the position of the buried person."

The guests split into pairs to practise hiding and finding transceivers, making sure the transceivers they have hidden are transmitting. Ruedi and I coach the individuals on their technique. Once everyone has practised, we gather back up in a large group. Ruedi says, "Now we will talk about what to do if involved in an avalanche. When going uphill it is important that you are not wearing safety straps attached to your skis. It makes getting rid of your equipment impossible.

With skins on you'll not be able to slide out of the avalanche. Any skis that you are wearing will only drag you down. If you are skiing downhill, try to identify a safe place out of the path of the slide and ski to it. If you know you are caught and there is no way out, yell loudly to draw attention to where you are, jettison your gear, then you must fight to stay on the surface. This will be hard – you will be fighting for your life. Once the snow comes to a stop and you're buried, try to determine if some part of you is on the surface and then wiggle it. If nothing is above the snow, try to move your body a bit to compress the snow in order to build a bigger air pocket around your body and then relax." The group listens with rapt attention to Ruedi's description of being in an avalanche. Each person seems to go through the steps in his or her mind.

Then 21 people with skis on trample out a large area in the snow to mimic avalanche debris. Ruedi buries two transmitting units placed in stuff sacks to protect them from getting wet and snowy. The aim is to use a large group to find two buried units.

Before the simulation exercise, Ruedi talks about the coordination required in larger emergencies: allocation of human resources and equipment, radioing for help, head counts, approaching the subjects, placing rescuers safely on the site. Then we practise. We all line up facing north and spaced about four metres apart. As one massive line, we march along the site with our transceivers in receive mode as the members of the group hone in on the buried units. Within a couple of minutes, we find both transceivers.

After the training, Ruedi reviews information on burial times by saying, "The longer someone is buried, the less chance they have of survival – it is just that simple. We have to be quick to respond. If a person is buried for 30 minutes, statistically they only have a 50 per cent chance of survival. If we rescue a person who was buried with their head below the surface, they will be flown out to the hospital. That's what we do." His presentation is informative and professional.

With the Avalanche Beacon School completed, we pull out our lunch. I take a few bites of my salami sandwich and wash it down with some sweet licorice tea from my small, dented thermos. My eyes pan the group, seeking a friend, but I can't find the motivation to engage. I usually love connecting with the adventurers, but instead I find myself having lunch alone, feeling a chill come over my body. I make an assumption: everyone has come to ski with Ruedi.

After eating, we divide into groups. Ruedi says, "People who want to ski in the fast group need to stand over there on the left, and those who want to ski slower go over to the right with Ken." I collect my backpack and poles and slide over to join those gathered on the right. In the group are John, Jeff, Paula, Kathy, Dennis, Robyn, Eric Klostermann, Craig, Charles and Jean-Luc. Ruedi strides up next to us in his white pants and orange jacket and says, "You guys have it all wrong; this is my group. Ken, you are going over there to take that group in behind."

As if carefully trained to follow orders without question, I ski over to those who wanted to go fast – Dan, Heidi, Rick M., Rick R., Keith, Bruce, Evan, Naomi, Vern, Age and Joe – and say, "Well, folks, it looks like we're the second group. We all ski about the same speed anyway." The guests are baffled by the turn of events, some visibly disappointed. I wonder about what just happened, and even more about why I'd complied. The only thing that makes any sense to me is that Ruedi wants Craig in his group. Craig is a high-profile guest. But there is no way for me to be certain that this is Ruedi's motivation. My response to the group I'm left with seems lame to me; I do not know how to clarify the situation with them.

Ruedi double-checks that everyone's transceiver is back on transmit after our practice. We ski past him, then wait in our groups 70 metres away, so that he can take the lead again, up from the soccer field and on toward Moon Hill Knoll. Ruedi's group moves in front and mine follows 50 to 100 metres behind, as I have been instructed. My skins glide with a slight resistance on the snow, sounding like fingers sliding on a middle guitar string. Projecting her voice over the sound of our skis, behind me on her telemark skis, Naomi asks, "Ken, have you been guiding here long?"

"No, this is only my third week up here. I've guided other places, like Yamnuska and Island Lake Lodge, and I just finished this fall working at the University of Calgary. It was the last field session of the Outdoor Pursuits route in kinesiology. I was a sessional instructor there," I answer sheepishly.

"So you're from Calgary?"

"Originally yes, but my wife, Nancy, and I just built a home here in Revelstoke this past summer. What about you?" I say, glancing over my shoulder to see her striding up the track in her yellow coat.

"I just finished my degree in chemical engineering at the U of C this last spring. I've done some work in the outdoors – mostly water-based stuff. I've worked at Churchill River Canoe Outfitters, Nahanni Wilderness Adventures and the Rocky Mountain Paddling Centre."

"Ah, Randy," I say, dropping the owner's name. "He's a good man. You must know him?"

"Yeah, I know Randy – he's a character!"

"We both worked on the Yamnuska semester program. I was involved with mountain programs and Randy instructed the ten-day paddling programs with the students." I try to carry on this conversation while still paying diligent attention to where we are going. There is a high overcast and we can easily see the key features of the snow-blanketed mountains. I try to establish some ease in conversing with Naomi, but it eludes me. Wracked by my insecurities I fear that Naomi can hear the tension in my voice, and as we carry on, she seems less interested in our conversation. After a while, we stride up the mountain in silence.

We ascend past Moon Hill Knoll, a miniature height of land between alpine valleys. Cresting the ridge, we ski on towards Woolsey Peak; a long, arching track takes us right to the top. Our two groups gather in the large wind scoop at the top of the run that leads north down into Boogie Basin, west of the height of land we had just traversed. The air fills with laughing, conversation and the clicking of gear as we strip off our stick-on skins and adjust our equipment for going downhill. I am in my own space, viewing the world through a bubble.

After giving directions for three-turn spacing, Ruedi launches down the slope on his snowboard, confidently shredding the snow, attacking the fall-line; after he rides three turns, I signal to the next person to go. With his ten people at the bottom, I follow suit with my group and enjoy beautiful powder turns down onto the flats far below. Reaching the bottom, I see Joe and Age still at the top, working on Age's gear. They get the equipment issue sorted out, then ski and ride down to the group. Finally, we proudly look up at the tracks we have laid down the mountain. I pull my skins out of my pack and go through the process of pasting them back on and adjusting my equipment for going uphill again. The guests know the drill and follow suit. Ruedi begins setting track, pointing his splitboard skis further from the chalet towards Elm Peak. I look at my watch, sense the waning light and realize that we will be staying out a little longer than we have on other first days this season. Equipment ready, each of us in turn follows the well-set track. In moments, we fall into a single line of two groups elegantly climbing the mountain.

I struggle to keep my group far enough away from Ruedi's. The slower skiers in the front group string themselves out in a very long line, some struggling to keep pace with their leader. Gauging my stride off the members of my group and the need to stay behind Ruedi's group is challenging. The pace I pick is still too fast, and our groups grow closer.

The terrain rears gradually to become the side of Elm Peak; the light diffused as we move into the shady northeast side of the mountain. The air is cooler in the shadow, and I feel the chill. I nip at the tails of Kathy's skis – the last person in the front group – and our two groups coalesce into one. She has long, dark hair that comes out of her toque in a braid and rests on her purple coat.

Kathy is fit and easygoing. I notice she is having some trouble negotiating the kick turns on the steep track heading up to the summit. The wind has pressed the snow into very hard "Styrofoam" on the ridge, so her skins don't grip as easily as they could. I say, "Hold your skin flat against the snow without edging – it'll grip better." She teeters during one of the kick turns she makes as the track Ruedi laid down makes an acute angle to face the other direction. With steep rocky terrain below on the south side of the ridge, I slide in to spot her. She seems to appreciate the effort. As we ascend, I promise to coach her kick turns when we have a safer place to do them.

A wave of concern washes over me as the track pushes out to touch the northeast face. While it seems quite safe here, I recognize that with so many of us skiing in such close proximity, an avalanche could catch quite a few of us. I also feel nervous about the wind effect in the northeast bowl that we are about to ski. I harbour these thoughts as the steep terrain gives way to a bright low-angle ridge near the top of the mountain.

On top of Elm Peak, I weave my way through the large group to talk to Ruedi. The vast expanse of the Selkirks looms around us: to the south the terrain drops off steeply to a deep treed valley far below; to the north, through the clouds, a heaving sea of peaks stretches as far as the eye, and even the imagination, can see. When I reach him, he says angrily, "I saw you back there helping that woman in my group. Don't baby them. They'll figure it out. If you baby them, they'll need babying. I told you that last week."

I say nothing in response, but frustration wells up inside me. In the 20 years I have been at the outdoor game I have never experienced this kind of treatment by a co-worker. Fully certified as an alpine guide, I am nevertheless being treated like a beginner in the business here. Feeling a need to share my perspective, I say, "You know it was really crowded on the way up here. There are too many of us too close together. I think I should be on a different peak altogether." Just then one of the guests asks Ruedi a question, taking his attention elsewhere, so he doesn't come back to acknowledge my comment. I am made to feel invisible, irrelevant. Inside, the pit returns to my stomach and I take myself back into my cave.

The group looks like a retail store full of multi-coloured Gore-Tex that shifts and crinkles as we all get ready to ski the Northeast Bowl. I know that it is a lee slope and the latest wind event may have built a slab of transported snow onto this wind-protected bowl, just like snow densely drifting in behind fences on the Prairies, creating the conditions for an avalanche. I also think about the rain crust far below us, the result of a warm November storm that had brought early winter rain to the tops of all the peaks, and is now still lying like a tilted skating rink near the bottom of the snowpack we are on. My mind drifts back to a party at Larry Dolecki's place three weeks ago with a number of guides in attendance. A group of us were discussing the snowpack when Norm Winter said, "That layer of rain crust scares me, and it will probably terrify me for the rest of the season."

Filled with these thoughts and emotions, I watch Ruedi give directions to the group. "Dere will be some wind effect on the top of the snow in this bowl. So I want you to ski this one at a time, alternating on either side of my track." I breathe a sigh of relief, thinking, *At least we'll ski it one at a time; if the slope avalanches only one person will be caught instead of the whole group.*

I slide to a spot on the ridge where I can view the

guests as they ski and ride the slope. My position will help me respond if something happens.

Ruedi glides onto the slope, probing the snow with his ski pole. He pushes a line out into the bowl to check the conditions and comes back. Then, pointing his board down the fall line, he rides the slope, confident and without incident. I watch the lead group ski or ride next to Ruedi's line one by one, alternating right and then left of his track. After his group has descended, I give the same directions to my group, slide into the bowl and ski the line.

Using my skis as a sensory organ, I feel the snow below me for signs of instability. It has the wind-drift skin on it, but it is not a thick enough slab to concern me. I think as I ski, *There isn't enough mass to this drifted snow to be affected by gravity.* But I know there are more issues with the snowpack than just this surface assessment. Halfway down the slope I come to the part that has been sheltered from the wind, find better snow there, and relax, enjoying the turns. With the elevation remaining, I point my skis straight so I glide out to the flats some distance away from the face to where Ruedi has gathered the others.

Once stopped, I turn to face the slope; I swing my ski pole in the air to signal the next person to start the descent. Although I have rationalized the conditions, I hold my breath as each of my group members comes down one at a time. One person falls and I cringe; a wipeout puts more stress on the snow at a single point.

That point of stress could be the thing that releases the slope. In a few anxiety-affected minutes, everyone joins us at the bottom.

With happy skiers gathered around, we look back at our tracks on the snowy face. The lines, more jagged and angular on the top third of the slope in the wind-affected snow, become nicely rounded and controlled at the bottom. Then we wait for some members of my group to put their skins on in preparation for the short climb back to the top of Moon Hill. After the last skiers adjust their gear, we climb up a short distance around the north side of Moon Hill, strip our skins and ski the gentle rolls most of the way back to the chalet.

At the bottom Evan and Joe talk about how they nearly collided on the run. I think about how I did not stress spacing out enough to avoid crashes with other skiers in my group. We skin up and make the last short climb up to the chalet. Outside the building, I count heads to be certain that we have everyone. With all accounted for I make a beeline for the staff accommodation on the north side of the chalet and change into a pair of jeans and a T-shirt.

Sliding on a down jacket, I feel more comfortable in the cold room. I take three deep breaths. I feel my stress melt at the end of each breath, but it overtakes me again in a moment. "Just stand up to him," I say aloud to myself. I think back to all the previous SME employees I had talked to before coming to work here myself. There were very few who had enjoyed it. However, I also know that other guides had been able to manage their situations. "I wonder what they have as people that I don't seem to have," I ask myself. The word "easygoing" comes to mind for both of the people I remember having said they'd had no problems. But as hard as I try, I can't let go and see past the conflict that seems to hover over my perception of this place. Ruedi's comments from today overtake my being, and my thoughts race like a runaway train. I replay each comment repeatedly in my mind – mostly: "You have it wrong." "Don't baby them."

Reluctantly, I slide into my felt-lined winter boots and amble over to the separate building that serves as both the Beglingers' home and the office to attend our evening guides' meeting. I open the door, step inside and take my boots off. Clear across the toasty-warm room, I see Ruedi watching TV with his young girls cuddled up around him. Charlotte is the older of the two, blonde and lanky; Florina looks more like her mother, with darker hair. Ruedi looks peaceful and gentle. After getting up, he finds a six-pack of hard apple cider stored under the stairs and hands me one as he walks over to the briefing table. Encircled by run photos on the walls, I sit down, crack open the cider and take a long pull of the sweet beverage. I feel the stress that is in every muscle of my body melt as the alcohol courses through my vessels. I joke to myself, "I can't even taste the alcohol."

Jean-Luc enters the office room to ask Ruedi about a ski issue he is having. It is clear to me that they are old friends, since Ruedi stands up, greets him warmly and calls him Lucci. He is a big man with dark hair, a moustache and an ever-present smile on his face. Lucci had cut his skiing teeth in Switzerland and for the past ten years has lived and worked at Engadine Lodge, in the Rockies closer to Calgary. Nancy and I used to take bike trips through Kananaskis Country and stay at Engadine, where he is the chef, so I know Lucci a bit. He is an amazing guy and I get up to greet him as well. Ruedi finishes his business with Lucci, who departs. As Lucci leaves, Jeff comes into the office, closes the door tightly, takes his boots off and joins us at the table. Jeff is on a practicum as part of his Association of Canadian Mountain Guide (ACMG) ski guide training, here to observe and learn from the guiding team. He is a blond-haired, fit young man who seems understated. He is keen to gather all the information he can about guiding and skiing, and in possession of a competence that shines through the surface.

Ruedi says, "Okay, let's fill out this operations book, ah? Here, Ken, you fill out the columns." He shoves the ledger-like book over to me across the table.

"Okay, 3 cm of new snow today, max temp minus four, min temp minus eight.[1] Height of snow 152 centimetres. We skied Moon Hill, Woolsey Peak and Elm Peak. No natural or skier-triggered avalanche observations today."

"Stability is Good below treeline, Good at treeline and Good in the alpine with some windslabs," Ruedi says.

“Ski quality … I think it was wind-affected on Elm,” I say.

“The skiing was excellent today. You don’t know bad snow,” Ruedi snaps.

We discuss some of the guiding skills that we used and their importance. Ruedi underlines how critical it is to create distance between the slope and the regroup spot after skiing it, saying, “If a slide happens while guests are skiing a slope, you don’t want to nuke your whole group by gathering too close to the bottom.”

After mustering up my courage, I tentatively add, “On that note, I think my group should be on a separate objective so that it’s not so crowded. There were too many of us up there on Elm Peak today. It made me nervous.”

Ruedi replies, “No, you don’t know the routes well enough yet. You follow 50 metres behind me.”

While I can agree that I don’t know the routes well, inside I feel that we are pushing our luck travelling so close together. Conflicted, I say, “Okay.”

After dinner and cleanup I head back to my staff accommodation at about 8:30 p.m. and make some notes. Ruedi had instructed me not to make notes in my field book during the day. I have always been poor at keeping notes, so I didn’t argue at the time, but I am making them now.

JANUARY 19, 2003

After a night of ruminating, I roust myself at 5:30 a.m.,

pull layers on one by one over my body and step outside. I walk over and see no new snow at the weather station. The temperature is -8.5 and there is a 150 cm HS (Height of Snow). In the brief morning guides' meeting, I learn that the plan for the day is to tour up and over Forbidden Peak and down to the west fork of Fang Creek. After breakfast, a few of the guests talk to Ruedi about being unhappy with the groups they are in and he reshuffles some of the slower-moving people to my group in an effort to make balanced teams. Robyn, Paula, Eric and Kathy shift into my group, while Age, Evan, Naomi and Heidi move into Ruedi's.

Before going skiing, I walk over to the living room with a cup of tea in hand and hear Dennis playing guitar. While strumming lightly, he converses in soft tones with a few of the others. When there is a break in the dialogue, I say, "So ... you're not skiing today, Dennis?"

"No, my knee's a little sore. I'll just hang out here today," he answers. Dennis is soft-spoken and gentle and his supple guitar-playing gives the chalet a warm, relaxed feel. He wears glasses, has a salt-and-pepper beard and long, sandy-coloured hair that is thin on top. I converse with him briefly and learn that he is a telemark ski instructor in California and lives with his wife, Carol, in Los Angeles. I note that he seems like an old soul who is comfortable in his own skin. I envy the day he has planned for himself and his freedom to choose. Turning my shoulders from the cozy situation, I stroll away and get myself prepared for my day, grabbing my jacket and well-ordered pack from my room, still thinking about Dennis. While waiting for the others to gather outside, I demonstrate a few kick turns for Kathy and coach her on them so that she is better able to negotiate the switchbacks on steep sections of track. She says, "I'm so happy to be in your group today. I don't want the pressure of having to go so fast."

"Thanks, Kathy," I respond. Inside I sense that Kathy has a naïveté about her. The Selkirks are a very different range from those of her home in the Sierra Nevada. Her open, easygoing attitude about her surroundings makes me wonder if she understands the severity of skiing in this terrain. It seems she trusts Ruedi and me implicitly for her safety. I feel unnerved, but say nothing.

Heidi says, "I'll miss skiing with you, Kathy – have fun!"

"You have fun too. We'll hang out after and have a few," Kathy says.

Nicoline steps out of the chalet, ready to ski. She doesn't come out with the guests every day, but when she does, she seems happy. I wonder if having her along will affect the day, if Ruedi will mellow in her presence. I test everyone's beacon as each person, in turn, slides out to the flats southeast of the chalet.

Shortly after leaving, we ascend a steep series of mushrooming snow pedestals supported by narrow rock ledges through which Ruedi skilfully sets the track up to Mirror Lake. At the top of the ledges, I identify a problem and speak to Ruedi about it over the radio. "Hey,

Ruedi. Robyn seems to be having a tough time keeping up. Her stride is short and her pace about one-quarter that of the others in my group. I think she's tired from yesterday."

Ruedi replies, "She's fine, I have guided her before and she's strong, no problem."

Thinking his rationale invalid because he is basing it on her performance last year and not her present situation, I persist. "The pace I have to set to match hers is too slow – it's difficult for the rest of the guests to maintain; people are getting cold and antsy. This is a good spot for her to turn around, since we're still close to the chalet."

"No, Ken," Ruedi replies with a tone of frustration. "You have to guide her. A good guide is able to manage the people he gets in his group." We carry on for a few minutes, then take a break just before skiing onto the Durrand Glacier itself. There I check in with Robyn and say, "How're you doing? It seems like you're struggling a little bit," trying to hide the stress I'm feeling because of the pressure I sense from the faster skiers still in my group.

Robyn answers with agitation in her voice, "I'm fine, I can do this, there's nothing wrong with me."

"Where're you from, Robyn?" I ask.

"Seattle," she says.

"It'll take you a couple of days to get adjusted to the thin air. We'll keep moving." She gives me a look of defiance, as if I have humiliated her by being honest about how slowly she is ascending. We carry on and I position her right behind me so she has the psychological advantage of having the group push her forward. During the climb up the glacier, I feel frustration wax inside me. I tell myself, *I am unable to act on a choice I know in my heart is the right one.*

Our glacial trudge finally brings us the summit of Forbidden Peak, and Ruedi's group is nearly ready to depart. The plan is for the two groups to ski further away from the chalet, down 2,900 feet to the 5,800-foot elevation on the west fork of Fang Creek. I don't think Robyn can manage – not only the ski down, but also the long slog back up from that far down. I am worried about pushing Robyn too hard and having her injure herself a long way down in Fang Creek, or on the ski home. I take Ruedi aside to speak with him and say, "Ruedi, she's terribly slow and has very low energy. I don't think it's safe for her to ski down there."

Ruedi responds, "If you are a good guide you can get her through it."

Dejected, I leave Ruedi's side and move back to my group.

With the features of the slope disappearing in the flat light of a white mist, we ski down into the depths of Fang Creek. Robyn falls repeatedly during the first pitch of the descent. After each crash, I fear that she will not get up. My mind plays through the scenarios. The weather is not flyable for a rescue. It is plain to me that it would be impossible to pull her on a sled all the way back to the chalet. I envision camping out with her if she is injured. I also fear that if something happens to her, I will have the full burden of responsibility laid upon me; I am beside myself with frustration. My 20 years of managing people in the mountains keeps telling me that I am pushing her too much. I witness many more falls. Rick Reynolds takes Robyn under his wing and skis slowly right in front of her so that she is able to see the terrain. I need to be out front in order to find the way in the flat light.

Skiing down at our tedious pace, we reach the lunch spot at 5,800 feet only moments before Ruedi wraps up his break with his group and begins skinning back up. With the cloud ceiling dropping, he climbs past my group, too far away for us to talk face to face. He makes no effort to check in with me, nor do I with him. After he has passed, I realize that I want to set up a collection point. I try to communicate with him, but his radio makes a low-battery squeal. I think, *He must have not put his unit in the charger last night.*

I feel pressure from all sides. I need to give my guests a good break here and, being a new guide in this terrain, I also know that if it whites out and I lose the lead guide's track in the snow and wind, it will take even longer to get home. We are not working together – Ruedi is controlling the decision-making, but the consequences are mine to live with. I have the group eat a quick lunch, then we paste our skins on our skis and stride one foot in front of the other uphill. I manage Robyn carefully en route up the 2,900 feet back to Durand Gendarme and Durrand Col, setting a slow, steady pace. Behind me, I sense the frustration of the group; they would like to go faster. I see Keith Lindsay in back with his dark beard, swinging his arms to generate enough heat, something he wouldn't have to do if we went faster. The weather closes in as we gain height.

Every few minutes I check our elevation on my watch altimeter. Ruedi's track begins to come in and out of view in the blowing snow. I scrutinize the slope aspect with my compass and mark my position on the map. Through the mist, I can see the rocky northeast shoulder of Forbidden Peak and I use it as a signpost to find my way back to the summit and on towards Durrand Col, where I hope that Ruedi and his group are waiting.

We arrive at Durrand Col to find no sign of the lead group. I think, *Had I known I would be on my own I could have made better whiteout preparations for the trip down.* I feel the sting that the complacency of following a lead guide can bring when things do not go according to plan. I decide to follow Ruedi's group's now faint tracks descending the glacier and back to the chalet via the 7,910-foot-level traverse. This traverse travels west off the glacier and retraces our steps back past Mirror Lake and down several steep ledges.

Before we begin skiing, I say, "We can't afford to lose one of you in this fog. It would at very least mean a cold night for you. We have to stay close together and ski slowly." I make eye contact with everyone, and each of their goggled faces nods in agreement. I wipe condensation from my eyewear so that my view is as clear as possible and turn from the group to ski down the track that comes in and out of view through the blowing snow. The cold bites my cheeks as I gain speed, the wind blowing from left to right drifts snow that obliterates more and more sections of the track. I am mindful that I need to relax so that my body absorbs the bumps. The only sensory input I have is the feel of the ground under my skis; I now discern no features visually.

I take a compass bearing on the track to keep our general direction correct. I am reticent to commit to a bearing directly to 7,910, because it will slow us down to properly travel on a bearing. I choose the faster descent down the ski track but fear losing sight of it completely. I stop every 100 metres to let people catch up.

I look back to count ten members of my group and see Robyn fall yet again, increasing my level of stress. Rick helps her get up and I am thankful for his assistance and compassion. Down the slope I continue, the sense of urgency building as I visualize the storm worsening. The next time I check my altimeter I am at 7,800 feet, under the 7,910-foot level, 100 feet below the west exit off the glacier. Damn! "*I can't believe you did that!*" I say to myself. The white clears enough for a moment for me to see the notch. Without letting on about my mounting stress to the guests, I think: *I do not have a group that can go uphill anymore.* Looking at my snow-dusted, laminated map, I decide to abandon my original plan and head home via Goat Lake. I comfort myself with the idea that it is a better choice with such a weak skier. Going down these now trackless steep hummocks would be inviting disaster.

The group gathers around and I check in with them. Robyn says she is fine but her face tells a different story; it is ashen. We carry on down the glacier, skiing in a white world, aiming for the western edge, where I find a few more features that allow some depth perception. On the windswept glacial moraines, I am able to see more because the black rocks give depth to the white landscape, but I fear that my skiers will find a shallow part of the snowpack, hit hidden rocks there and fall. I slow the group even more to compensate and protect them. I count heads as we reach a flat spot I suspect to be near Goat Lake. Using my GPS, I confirm our position just south of the lake. Though it is challenging, I am connecting the dots on the return home. A call comes in from Ruedi on the chalet radio.

"Where are you?" He speaks in a slow, laconic voice without any greeting.

"Near Goat Lake," I say.

"Fuck." He responds flatly. After a long pause, he says, "What's your grid reference?"

I try to move away from the group so that they can't hear any more abusive transmissions, but the guests just follow me wherever I go. After checking both the map and my GPS, I say, "327796."

"Okay," he says, half-regaining his patience, "from there you will ski due north until you find the boulder."

I take a deep breath, reel in my composure after the near panic of being abused in front of my group, and ski north with compass in hand dialled to 360, my band of skiers following me. Within half an hour, and confirming my position several times with an impatient Ruedi, we ski, albeit carefully, down the slope just east of the chalet as dusk falls. On the last slope, Robyn crashes numerous times, struggling to get up after each fall. I see the frustration in her movements. Rick continues to selflessly help her down the last slope. I pick the route and lay a reference track for them to use as a guide rail. When we finally arrive at the chalet, everyone is tired of, or from, something. I see a conglomeration of expressions on the collection of faces, relieved that nobody is hurt. Few are happy about the day. For me it has been a day with a much higher level of risk than I am comfortable with as a guide. I feel defeated and frustrated all at once as I prepare myself for Ruedi, certain that he will berate me in some way the moment I step in the door. Sweeping all of the snow off myself I walk into the chalet. Ruedi hands me a cold cider and is surprisingly cheerful, saying, "There's no guides' meeting tonight; I have to work on the electrical system." I feel relieved for the short term, but I now have to wait longer for what I know is coming.

Dinner is a welcome comfort after a difficult day. I wash dishes afterward, sharing good camaraderie in the kitchen with Dave Finnerty. Dave is the nanny for Charlotte and Florina. He's also here to shovel snow for the whole winter and help out wherever needed around the chalet in exchange for a number of days of skiing a week. He is of medium height and build with short dark hair, and he gets along with everyone including Ruedi. I envy his popularity.

With a dishtowel in hand, he tells his "diesel fitter" joke, about two former women's underwear manufacturers collecting unemployment insurance. One gets twice the compensation because he's categorized as a skilled labourer. The other gets the minimum allowance as a garment worker. The more highly compensated one tells the employment insurance agent that he is a "Diesel Fitter." His work is therefore classified as skilled labour and insured at a higher rate. But his only task in the factory was to place the underwear on his head and say, "These will fit her." It feels good to laugh.

At 8:30 p.m. my day finally ends. I go over to the staff accommodation to get some rest. I feel as undercompensated and undervalued as the straight-talking garment worker myself after 15 hours of hard labour and with people's lives in my care. What do I have to say or do to get on a higher side of value in my life, I wonder as I arrive in my quarters, light the fire in the small cast-iron wood stove, brush my teeth, lay out my equipment for morning and slide into an ice-cold bed.

CHAPTER 2

BURIED

JANUARY 20, 2003

At 4:30 a.m. I roll out of bed with a sense of foreboding after another sleepless night. My lower back is stiff from the ten days of ski touring I have already done on this shift. My feet touch the freezing cold floor of the staff accommodation and I flinch. The knot of anxiety is much worse today. I even recoil from the thought of brushing my teeth, because the very act will bring me one step closer to facing the day. Is the stress of working with Ruedi bothering me, or is it the fear of what I know about this winter's snowpack? Once again I choose to focus on Ruedi, obsessing about every petty little thing about him. I splash my face with cold water, trying to shrink the bags under my eyes. I tell myself I will make it to Friday and then quit working here. I suppress the voice telling me to do it now because that would be giving up. I pull on my armour, a blue synthetic top, step into my tan pants, thread into my orange windshirt and don a brightly striped toque before heading outside.

Tiny snowflakes flash across my headlamp beam piercing through the black early morning. One centimetre of snow has accumulated overnight. I start the task of clearing the deck with a big sliding shovel. Through the darkness I see Dave, partially illuminated by light from the chalet, grab one of the scoop shovels from the hooks on the wall and join me on the east side. After saying good morning, I ask him, "How do you do it, Dave?"

"How do I do what?" he asks.

"Get along with Ruedi?"

"He can be difficult at times, especially when he's in one of his moods. I just look past it to see the good parts."

"I just can't seem to do that. I had a particularly rough day yesterday with him. He totally disregards what I think should be done. I'm not sure I'm going to last working here."

"Everyone has their good side, but I can understand how he could be difficult to work with. He's mostly good to me."

"I can't seem to keep him from getting under my skin. I'm deeply affected by his comments."

"Yeah, I understand. I can see how hard he is on others, but for some reason he's okay with me. Maybe it would be different if I were a guide. I guess he just has less to get after me about," Dave says.

We finish shovelling in silence. I walk over to the weather station and record −7°C, broken cloud, light north winds and 1 cm of new snow on the board.[2] The total height of snow, I note, is 148 centimetres.[3]

Ruedi, Jeff and I meet in the office to finish our guides' meeting from the day before. We talk about the change in route that I took from 7,910 to Goat Lake.

Ruedi says, "All you needed to do was follow my track. Can't you even do that?"

"Well, with the new snow, the wind and the whiteout conditions, I was unable to see the track that you had made at least an hour before. It was like being inside a Ping-Pong ball out there. I overshot the traverse to 7,910 by a hundred feet."

"Ping-Pong ball? You Canadian guides, what the hell does the ACMG teach you anyhow? There was no whiteout yesterday!! All you had to do was follow the track!! It was easy."

Trying to remain calm I say, "I could see the notch at 7,910 in and out of the clouds. All that was required was to put our skins back on and climb up. Robyn was too tired to do that, so I dropped down to Goat Lake. And another thing, Ruedi: I don't think that swearing on the radio is appropriate. It can easily unsettle our guests."

Pacing around the room like a caged animal, waving his arms, Ruedi barks, "That was not bad language!! You have not heard me use bad language yet!!!"

"Your language was inappropriate for the radio." There is silence – then Ruedi lets go of it. My mind flashes to his scrambler setting on the radios and why he wants nobody to hear what is going on up here.

We record the previous day's observations in the office logbook; rate the snow stability as "Good in the subalpine, Good in the lower alpine, Good with partial windslabs in isolated areas in the higher alpine,"[4] reflecting the southwest winds yesterday afternoon. I feel like the stability rating we have given seems generous, but I have not seen any recent avalanches. So I say nothing, but my gut flips. When we finish, I ask, "Where are we going today?"

"We'll go over to Swiss Meadows, then to Fronalp and then La Traviata," he says. The meeting is over and Ruedi leaves for the chalet.

I pull out the run photos and the map and pore over them for some time until I have an understanding of where we are skiing, my pulse still pounding from the exchange with Ruedi. Then I walk over to put together my lunch with everyone else.

While we are doing this, it becomes clear that some people slated for my group today are still not happy about being in the slower group. There are individuals who want to go hard and are taking this week very seriously. The intensity of the whole group is daunting to me – few are willing to just go with the flow and see what the week presents. The few people that are relaxed seem to be having more fun. Ruedi indicates that he will do what he can to reconstitute the groups and leaves the issue until he knows how many people would like the day off, which could affect the overall numbers and give us more flexibility.

I sit down with my bowl of homemade Swiss-style muesli at the head of the table by the door. As Craig sits down next to me I ask, "How was your day yesterday?"

"It was good – flat light, but good. How was yours?"

"Oh, it was tough. It was slow going. We got in late," I say.

"Yeah, I noticed. It's hard work sometimes."

"It is. So you're thinking of doing the guiding thing, Craig?"

"Yeah, working towards it, ... I was just on my Level 2 Avalanche Course last week and enjoyed it a lot. I especially learned a lot from the instructors on our days in the field.

"It is a long road," I offer.

"Where are you in the process?" he asks.

"I'm a full Alpine Guide and an Assistant Ski Guide. I have one more exam to complete in the spring, then I'll be a full guide if I pass. I came up here to get a bunch of ski touring experience under my belt, which should make a big difference. But so far, I have mostly focused on climbing in my career. How about you?"

"I'm here as part of my practicum. I'm working towards becoming an Assistant Ski Guide."

"Do you intend to take your exam on a snowboard?"

"Yeah, I do. I'm most comfortable with a board."

"Well, of course you are."

"Do you have a plan after working here, Ken?"

"I'm not sure what the future will bring for me. It's tough being away from Nancy a lot," I say.

"Yeah, I hear you, but I think I have a plan that will work. I don't want to be away from family much either."

"If you can work that out, you'll be doing well. Ruedi seems to have a formula that works for his family."

"Hey, what's that shirt you're wearing?"

"I don't know – something by Marmot, obviously. Ruedi gave me all of the clothes I need for work, but I have no clue what the name of this is. I love it, though. It's the best light layer I've ever toured in – it stops the wind but breathes really well. It's okay when it's snowing lightly, too."

"Hmm, thanks. I'll ask Ruedi about it and see if he knows."

"Yeah, he should know."

I gather our empty bowls and take them to the kitchen.

Ruedi briefs the group: "You don't need your skins on because we will be skiing down from the chalet to Twin Falls on our way to Swiss Meadows. Be very careful to put your skins in your pack. It would not be good to arrive at the bottom of the hill at Cairns Creek without your skins with you for the day. The snow down there will not be as good. There will be a temperature crust at that elevation."

With the briefing complete, I walk over to the office and have one last look at the run book to review our objectives. I feel more ill at ease than on the previous days and feel like I need more information, yet I am afraid to talk to Ruedi about this. I take a couple of the photos out of an old "ski run photos" book and put them in my chest pocket for reference.

Ruedi comes storming into the office, obviously furious about something. I realize it has to do with me when he shouts, his face throbbing red and his veins distending on his neck: "Craig just asked me about Marmot and the shirt you are wearing! Why the hell don't you know about this equipment I gave you?! Marmot sponsors me and SME, and it is very important that we all know what we are wearing!"

With my heart racing, I defend myself: "But you didn't tell me I was responsible for knowing about this stuff when you gave the equipment to me, nor did you provide me with any information about it."

When Ruedi offers no response, I ask, "So what's this shirt called and what are its qualities?"

My question meets with silence; Ruedi just walks away. I leave the office, shaking my head in frustration, and finish getting ready for the day. While packing I think, *I want to leave this place, but I'm afraid. It was my idea to move to Revelstoke with Nancy. We have a new house and now a new mortgage. I have to make this work somehow.*

The air is full of the clicking of equipment, the telling of dirty jokes, and responses of laughter – some uncomfortable, some with disgust – as we prepare to slide down to Cairns Creek. I check transceiver functions and that people have their skins in their packs.

With everyone ready, Ruedi says, "Okay, we need

to sort some groups out. I will take Heidi, Naomi, Charles, Age, Evan, Craig, Jean-Luc, Paula, Jeff, Joe and Dave when he finishes his chores and catches up to the group."

Left over for my group are Vern, Bruce, Keith, Rick M., Rick R., John, Dennis and Kathy. I make a mental note that Robyn, Dan and Eric have decided to take a rest day at the chalet.

Sliding off the edge of the platform where the chalet is perched changes our world. There is a great energy in the group, a brilliant playfulness as we descend the simple slope to Cairns Creek. The terrain has no avalanche risk, so I relax and enjoy myself, feeling the simple thrill of skiing again.

At the base of Twin Falls on Cairns Creek, 20 of us put our skins on, splashes of colour standing in the snowy valley bottom. The mountains rear up steeply to the north and east, and the Cairns Creek valley falls away to the west down to the Columbia River north of Revelstoke. Bruce, Keith, Rick and Rick slide over to Ruedi and I see them conversing about something. I understand what they want when Ruedi responds by sending Paula and Jeff to my group. Joe volunteers to shift as well so that the groups are balanced.

Musical frickin' chairs, I think to myself, shaking my head. Without my field book I make a mental note of which people I have in my group, reminding myself that head counts are critical for responding to an avalanche incident. Simplifying the process, I focus on the numbers twelve and eight, which will change by the addition of one to Ruedi's group once Dave catches up.

Ready to go, Ruedi says, "The track may go up and down a bit because of the alders on this side of the valley." He radioes the chalet and says, "We are en route from Twin Falls to Fronalp." Rotating his body 180 degrees, he slides over to Cairns Creek, pulls out his shovel and, with a few deft swipes of his blade, improves the snow bridge that crosses the creek.

Turning to my group, I say, "We have a long climb ahead of us. Dress lightly even though it's snowing a little bit."

Ruedi presses the radio microphone button: "Have the guests sidestep down the snow bridge so they don't fall in the creek."

"Copy that," I say with frustration. My group follows and we sidestep down the snow bridge and across the creek. Looking to the right, I see Dave coming down the slope to Twin Falls from the chalet. Ruedi ascends up and to the left, breaking trail, and the two groups, spaced about a hundred metres apart, work up the alder-spotted avalanche run-out zones between 5,500 and 6,500 feet.

On a traverse section of the track, I see Age and Craig having a tough time with their splitboards on the hard-packed snow. Once they pass that section, I notice they have taken the edge off the track, creating a wash-out that will make it difficult for my guests to traverse the slope. To ease the difficulty, I make a slight detour that flattens out the track and eliminates any struggle for those behind.

Ruedi says over the radio, "Stay exactly in the track I set."

I don't respond, feeling myself shut down and embark on a dark spiral down into the bitter, angry depths of myself. Sullen, I stride uphill without passion, following for no other reason than because it is what I believe is expected of me. I probe several of the slopes along the route with the handle end of my ski pole in an effort to find surface instabilities. I note that the skiing will be bad at this point on the way down because the snow consists of sun crusts and old avalanche debris. I envision everyone doing a controlled snowplow on the way home – our effort seems a waste of time.

Dave catches up to us just as we negotiate the first drainage. His energy is already pushing him beyond my group with a focus on the lead group, keen to ride with Craig. I feel him seeking a passing point.

The sound of ski edges scraping icy snow fills the air as we scale old avalanche debris from a massive slide that had come off Tumbledown Mountain earlier in the season. There is a little snow on top of the debris, but not enough to set a better track – everyone slips and scuttles on their skis, seeking better grip with their skins. Ruedi works to lay in a track on the climber's right side of the drainage for a while and then moves to climber's left and on up into a grove of massive Engelmann spruce trees. Shortly after entering the forest, my group takes a short break, having climbed for an hour. I feel protected and relaxed among the fragrant 300-year-old spruce. Taking a drink from my Thermos, I feel soothing warmth enter my body.

Dave strides on ahead to catch up with Ruedi's group. There is a spring in his step as he passes us, shuffling his tiny skis, his snowboard mounted on his back and a smile glowing on his face. He is off to ride with Craig. I marvel at his freedom, born of letting people be who they are, including himself. Shouldering my load, I lead the others up the long, gentle grade that pledges to break into the white subalpine.

My group snakes up the track that negotiates the terrain through the slowly thinning forest. When I next hear Ruedi, he is radioing the chalet, "We are having a break to regroup at the bottom of Swiss Meadows." I catch a glimpse of Dave joining the resting lead group. Just before my group catches up, Ruedi radioes, "We are en route from the bottom of Swiss Meadows to Fronalp."

I reach the opening at the base of Swiss Meadows and step off the track to the right, to see that we need to wait for John for a while. I take a drink from my water bottle and as the cool fluid pours down my throat, all I can think of is turning around. My memory goes back to the poor snow profile work I did last week. I botched it while rushing under Ruedi's pressure. I have a Level 2 avalanche certification, but snow profiles have always challenged me – it is my current weakness. I do not have the mileage I would like at this stage of my career. I struggled with my Level 2 course, but met the standard by the end of the course. I also did not have a recording template the day I did the snow profile. I had a field book for that process, but my notes were a mess. At the time, Ruedi had only wanted me to gather information efficiently: as he yelled out the door every 15 minutes, furious that it was taking so long, my mind often went blank. The profile was useless, and so at this point I feel like we do not have enough information to make good decisions today.

A fog descends on me; I see the people in my group but I am barely able to speak. They seem far away, yet I am standing right beside them. I think, *If I were here alone I would turn around.* I picture myself in the summer sitting peacefully by a mountain lake and long for a simpler life with peace and freedom.

We are just above the treeline, there is a slight wind and it is snowing lightly, so I put on a light jacket and encourage the others to do the same. Clouds billow all around us, sometimes revealing parts of the terrain above but mostly surrounding us in milky white. With leaden legs and heart, I carry on uphill, pondering the prospect of skiing these rolling slopes below Tumbledown Lake in the whiteout. I picture the experience being akin to riding a motocross track while wearing a blindfold.

I sense a looming presence to my right and through the mist I catch glimpses of Tumbledown Mountain gaining mass and dominance beside me. The track Ruedi is setting is within range of avalanches that could pour off that mountain. I tell my group members to spread out five metres apart and comfort myself with the thought that during the last avalanche cycle some large slides had come down, clearing out a lot of potentially hazardous snow above. Probing the surface snow next to the track, I find the top 30 centimetres becoming light and skiable. My mind travels down through the snowpack to the deep instability lurking near the bottom. I had specifically asked Ruedi about the November rain crust last week and he seemed to have confidence that it was settling out and bonding with the mass of snow that lay on top. Apart from our students' results, we had only done two tests in the last week: my botched snow profile and Ruedi's quick look at the top of the Goat Face. We have not seen any natural or skier-triggered avalanches in the last week, and we have been skiing some big features, but these facts do not dispel my unease.

The lead group reaches a point just above Tumbledown Lake at 6,800 feet. I hear on the radio, "Durrand Glacier Chalet, this is Ruedi; we are at Tumbledown Lake having a tea break." He has been able to see my group through the mist at several points during our ascent, so I decide to keep off the radio. After a few minutes, I join his group, take my pack off, place it on the snow beside me and pull out my snacks and Thermos. My group members slowly arrive one by one and I encourage them to rest and have something to eat and drink. It is a good, safe flat spot where we can see some of the surrounding terrain. I point out Fronalp and Tumbledown to my guests as the clouds open up.

Tilting my head back and to the right I see the steep, rock-studded headwall of Tumbledown Mountain looming above us through the clouds to the northeast. The knot that has been in my stomach all week tightens as my eyes scan an ailing matrix of rock and snow above me, which comes in and out of view through the Selkirk winter mist. I rest in the comfort that we are going to Fronalp first because it seems like much gentler terrain. Perhaps we will gain some information over there that will help us re-examine our plan to ski La Traviata, a run that just won't sit right with me this morning. I look at Ruedi across the group of 21 people. As my gaze studies him I see only a man I despise; there is a gulf between us that I don't have the heart or the ability to cross. I look around at the rest of the group and see them all having a good time. I am in a bubble that only allows me to see the worst in Ruedi and I do not have the courage to pop it. Anxiety paralyzes me, halting conversation or connection with anyone in any way. Someone tells an off-colour joke and I laugh, but I'm acting, showing the group only what I think they want to see. I can't seem to get out of my funk.

Ruedi shoulders his pack, rotates his splitboard skis around and points them up-mountain. His powerful legs carry him smoothly uphill while his group members follow behind one by one as they become ready.

I look back at my group as it prepares for the next section and see that Vern is using retention straps that secure his skis to his legs. "Hey, Vern, we're headed into some big country; let's take those straps off. I wouldn't want your skis attached to you in an avalanche," I say.

"Okay," he replies with more than a hint of embarrassment.

After helping Vern remove his straps, I shoulder my pack and ski onward as he strides mere inches from my ski tails. "You know, Ken, I'm frustrated about being in the slower group. It's tough for me to go at this pace."

"Yeah, it's been difficult getting people into the right groups this week," I respond.

"I came here to be challenged, and moving in the slow group is not all that challenging."

I counter his intensity by offering a different perception. "Perhaps your challenge is to let go of it and learn to go slow?"

"I'm not so interested in that, Ken."

"I'll talk to Ruedi again tonight, and we'll see what changes we can make for tomorrow."

"OK."

We carry on in silence as the green comfort of the trees steadily drops below with each stride upward. When I see Ruedi make a rounded right turn with his up-track, heading towards La Traviata on Tumbledown Mountain, my stomach flips. I think, *NO! DON'T GO THERE!!* I call Ruedi on the radio, masking my distress. "Ruedi from Ken. Uhhh, where are we going?"

Ruedi replies, "We're going to La Traviata. I radioed that in to the chalet at the break!"

Picturing my orange and black pack sitting on the snow at the last break, the radio in the top lid, I understand why I did not hear the call. I depress the Push To Talk button on my radio, wanting to say, "I don't think we should go there." But all that comes out is a betrayal of myself when I say, "OK."

Ruedi and his group of 12 ascend below the humbling face of La Traviata and I follow with my seven guests. He works confidently with his skis tracking up the pristine, snowy slope from the looker's left side of La Traviata, taking a high-side approach that we have often talked about, because it reduces the exposure to the slope. This puts his group safely below the rock face on the left – a small but important island of safety.

From there, he builds a perfectly inclined ramp for our two groups to follow. I marvel at his track-setting precision. He reaches forward in front of his ski tips, aggressively probing the snow, searching for instabilities. It is clear that his guests know to space themselves three metres apart. I see them equidistant along the perfectly ascending track like beads on a string. After traversing the entire slope, he reaches a wind feature in the snow on looker's right, where he creates a switchback platform for the guests to kick turn on, so that they can face the other direction and continue to climb. He carries on up the slope, punching his snowboard skis 25 centimetres deep with each stride. Like an automaton, I follow the wide side approach to the stress-inducing slope.

Moments later, my group of clients stand safely stowed below a rock cliff on the inclined approach track to the snow-laden mountainside. From my position at the front, the situation presses in on me as if I am descending into deep water. I crane my neck to the left to see the lead group ascending the steep 300-metre slope. My gut flips. Easterly winds have deposited a snowdrift from right to left looking directly at the mountain. I imagine the metres-thick mound resting on the ice near the base of the snowpack. Rick, one of the clients in the group above, races between the switchback corners as he ascends. His head snaps side to side, up and down, conveying nervousness about his position. Others in the lead group confidently move upward on the impending grade. One by one, the upper group members crest the steep convex roll and reach the gentle slope above. I cringe as each passing pair of skis scores the surface of the convexity, where the snow is most under tension.

Behind me Vern says, "I don't like it ... being below the other group." I reply weakly, "Neither do I." My voice cracks from my dry throat. With a pit in my stomach, I pause, hoping that Vern has the courage to say what I don't. But there is now only silence behind me. I tell myself that I have no choice. With feigned confidence, I say, "Wait here and follow with three-metre spacing when I wave you onto the slope." My heart thumps in my chest as I stride forward, following the track that

Ruedi made only minutes ago. An insane war rages in my head. It is deadly quiet outside.

I use my ski pole to probe and sense the snow just as Ruedi did. It shows no indication of a surface instability. It feels solid. I look down the incline through the flat white light and see a concave feature at the bottom. I push the idea that it is a terrain trap from my mind. Instead I imagine the mass of snow sitting on the slope above, supported by this concavity. "It will keep it from sliding," I mumble to myself. I look again at the group above; their collective weight seems to have no effect on the snow and there are no apparent signs of stress due to their presence. I dig into the top edge of the ski track and isolate a thirty-by-thirty-centimetre block. A hand shear test in this block produces no alarming results. All of my actions seem choreographed, as if I am going through the motions for an audience like some trained animal. I wave my group onto the slope.

They start moving up the track towards me. The air feels like it does moments before a collision. I rush to the far right side of the slope, to the turning point in the track. "It's not too late to get out of here," I reason. From this side, the track forms zigzags up the steep grade. I make a kick turn by swinging my downhill ski around 180 degrees. Toes pointed in opposite directions, I shift my weight onto this new ski and face to the left. The other ski follows to match the first. The manoeuvre heightens the feeling of vulnerability. I can now clearly see my group one by one reticently expose themselves to the pitch. I improve the kick turn platform, stomping it flat for those behind me. My defiant body keeps moving upward. Fuelled by my discomfort, I race ahead towards the track that rises above my seven following people. My haste closes the vital gap between us and the looming lead group above. I realize this and slow my stride to a snail's pace, my careening mind tortured by my glacial movement. Walking on eggshells, I look up, envious to see Charles in a sprint for the safety of the top. I peer down to watch the last trusting party member commit to the sick situation.

With all of my ascending skiers completely engaged across the mountainside, a sudden percussive WHUMMPH sends a shock wave directly to my knowing gut. There is a desperate hope-filled pause before the snow starts sliding, cut short when someone above yells "AVALANCHE!!!" I roar it again to those below me. Cracks appear across the slope as the snow, once solid, begins to shift over the landscape and under my skis. I topple uphill onto my right hip, like a wineglass on a shifted table. I am lying on a deck-sized slab of snow accelerating down-valley. Snow-laden air rushes past my face, plastering coldness onto my skin. I witness two clients near the tail end of my group get hit broadside by a wall of cinder-block-density avalanche. It bowls them over, sending them hurtling headfirst down the slope. The last I see of them is their bright ski-bound legs floundering against a white backdrop.

My trained reflexes take over. Several frantic scissor

kicks with my skis release my left boot from its binding. The remaining ski drops off with one urgent stomp from my free foot. My poles are gone. Released from my equipment, I ride on the solid plate of snow within the tumbling chaos of the avalanche. Time slows. My senses heighten. The slab I am riding bends over the uneven terrain and fractures like a concrete patio in an earthquake. My legs and hips fall into the widening cracks that appear in it at random. As the snow continues to crumble into infinite churning blocks, I feel the suction of the roiling mix. I brawl for control and remain on the surface with a butterfly backstroke.

As the steep slope melds into the undulating valley, speed dwindles and the snow comes to rest. I am buried upright to my waist, facing the base of the valley. The metallic taste of adrenaline dries my mouth as I scan the mounds of shattered ivory blocks to the left and right for signs of life. There is nothing, then some slight movement on the right. Most of my group is under the snow. The fear of responsibility pounds through me as I picture digging myself out and helping the buried.

An intense hissing sound approaches from behind. Another wave of debris, from the steeper part of the slope above, hammers my backpack and pushes me forward. The mass buffets me in all directions before it suddenly stops. I feel no pain. Everything comes to an eerie, silent rest. The surface feels a long way away. My body is upright, limbs packed tight in avalanched snow as if in a plaster cast. I cannot move. There are no pressure points. I experience a weightless, floating sensation in a strangely protected cocoon. I can only turn my head a couple of degrees. My left hand and my face share a beach-ball-sized airspace – a sphere of hope. I smell the cold humidity. "I'm okay," I repeat to myself.

Light from above filters down through my snowy grotto, forming countless shades of blue and turquoise as it refracts through the varying thicknesses of lumpy snow. There may be a series of connecting air pockets leading to the surface but I cannot be certain. Thin areas in my clothing begin to produce cold, damp places at my lower back and my knees, neck and right wrist, but there is nothing I can do to fix the problem. I feel strangely calm and relaxed, as if it all were familiar. But my pulse and breathing suddenly race when my mind registers the words: "I'm BURIED."

I grapple for self-control. One of my ski tips is visible in the back of my air pocket. If I use it to pierce the surface of the snow above, I will draw attention to where I am. Close to my face, I pinch the red and white ski with my gloved hand. A minuscule lateral movement with my left wrist shifts the ski a few centimetres skyward. The binding and the curved ski tip jam in the snow, arresting my effort. The surface is impossibly far away. My lungs gasp from the effort and I let go of any thought of assisting in my own rescue. I picture the red transceiver in my right hip pocket. I hope it's transmitting my location to the others and they can reach me before I completely run out of air. I envision the hurried stress of the people left on the surface. My mind flashes to my clients; all of them are in this snowy catastrophe. I am their guide, helpless to assist them. A wave of grief overcomes me while I cycle mental images of the snow hitting them, their legs flailing as they remain attached to their skis. With these pictures rolling in my mind, my heart thumps. I breathe heavily and feel the air become lifeless. My lungs scream for oxygen. I gasp but can't satiate them. Panic looms closer. I have to surrender. I place my head on my left arm, feel the deep weariness in my body, embrace it and let myself pass out.

A painless slap across my numb left cheek germinates some awareness. I take a deep breath and slowly awaken from emptiness. Visual inputs are diffuse and half-focused, as if I am looking through a distant blue haze. My limbs are dead with cold; muffled and muted sounds register. More input comes in: people in coloured clothing, wielding shovels blurred by their rapid movement. I pry their names from my memory as they pass in front of my field of view. Age ... John ... Joe ... Ron.

Someone to my left speaks the words, "Ken, you've been buried for 30 minutes. We got to you quickly."

As I gaze in the direction of the speaker, trying to capture his name, a voice from somewhere deep inside me tells me it was 35 minutes. I wonder why this detail is important. The name of the man who spoke dawns; it is Dan.

My body tingles from head to toe while I recognize that the shovellers have moved massive amounts of snow to excavate me. Before me is an eight-foot-wide snow ramp that gently ascends from the depths of my pit to the surface of the debris like a concrete loading dock. From my near-grave, I can see the terminus of the avalanche debris and down to several helicopters that sit on the flats below. Rescuers move with wobbly purpose on snow piled in lumpy mounds.

I feel a foreboding. In the absence of knowing, I sense that what has happened is bad. I have awakened to a nightmare; tears are just below the surface, as are anger, shame and guilt. I work hard to keep a lid on it, to be strong.

Those with shovels continue to move snow from around my body. Rick digs right in front of me, and others behind him transport snow further away. Their effort is difficult for me to receive. The bottom of my jacket meets the snow, my legs still encased and out of view. In seconds I can see my knees, and I assume I can step out of the snow. I struggle and tug at my snow-rooted feet, but my attempt is too early; I am still immobile. A shovel blade hits my leg, and the pain confirms that I am not dreaming. The cuffs of my red and silver Dynafit boots come into view. I make another futile jerk with each foot, but they remain cemented. Two more shovel swipes and I am free.

Dan asks, "Can you walk on your own, Ken?"

I say, "No," feigning weakness because I want out of

this nightmare. To be able to walk would mean that I should help with the rescue. To help with the rescue is too much, I want nothing to do with this. With one man under each arm, they support me out of my pit and we stumble downhill towards the waiting helicopter. The churned, blocky snow is hard to negotiate even with assistance; each man in turn supports my mass and keeps me from falling. I realize I could not have gotten far without help after all.

As we move, my hesitant eyes look left and glimpse part of what is happening; what I see replicates my concept of a war zone. Three or four helicopters – some with spinning rotors, others shut down – sit at the misty white bottom of the slope, the air laden with the burned kerosene smell of their exhaust. I notice people dressed in what I recognize as uniforms; their interactions are purposeful, confident and solemn. Packs, skis and rescue equipment line the perimeter of the debris, a supply line for the needs of the emergency effort. The energy at the scene is one of battle and loss. I am a coward, unable to turn and face the reality behind me: a situation I know I played a part in creating.

The men coax me around the far side of the waiting navy blue helicopter with its nose pointed west. Ron McAllister, a guide from Selkirk Tangiers Heli Skiing, helps me into the back seat. He shouts above the thump, squeal and hum of the helicopter, to nobody in particular as if he is thinking out loud, "Ken needs someone with him in case he has any issues on the way out."

Jeremy Cox measures the crown fracture of the La Traviata avalanche on January 21, 2003.

Dan yells, "I'll go with him." He jumps in next to me and assists my feeble efforts to put on my headset and seat belt. In the span of minutes, I have lived polar realities, from being buried in snow to the comfort of a helicopter seat, and I feel disoriented: everything is moving both fast and slow. I sit in the seat and realize that our destination is the Revelstoke hospital.

Rotor blades slice through the Selkirk cloud and, as they gain speed and momentum, morph into a black disc above our heads. I hear Gerry Richard, the pilot, check in with his heliport in a calm, measured voice. The rotors pitch with a thump as they grab the air and lift. I see the skid leave the snowy ground below; we take flight and a weight comes off my shoulders. I have struggled deeply with being in this situation in the first place, and now I get to leave. Being a victim might be my escape from it, but part of me knows there is no easy way out of this one. I have no idea what to do with this knowledge.

We gain height in relation to the slope and I scan the scene but only register coloured blobs scattered across the snowscape. The route ahead is almost completely obscured; random rocks and trees link across sections of opaqueness to form a breadcrumb trail. Gerry's head pivots, connecting these fixed visual points to guide the machine down-valley and get us out of here intact. We are like a blind man counting sections on the sidewalk with his cane in order to know his location. If conditions get any whiter, we will lose the metaphorical cane and could crash.

In stress-protracted minutes, we reach the trees. The master behind the controls calmly keeps the helicopter close to the treetops to use them as a visual "handrail."

The chaos from the avalanche scene we have left behind floods back to me through the headset. Ruedi reports in his stress-filled voice, "Dave is dead." I weep without restraint, and mutter through lips that drip with tears as my head hangs low, "Dave's gone. What a loss." I visualize him earlier in the day, his movements filled with joy, catching up to our group after his morning chores. He overflowed with enthusiasm to spend the day snowboarding with Craig. I remember his radiant motion as he climbed the slope, past our group, to join Craig at the tail end of the lead group. To him, this was going to be the best day ever. I grasp for the essence that was Dave and feel the painful realization that he is now intangible. I ache with grief for the loss and become crippled with fear.

Wind buffets the machine, pushing and pulling it in erratic directions. The usually quick trip stretches as we inch down the west slopes of the Selkirk Mountains above the unseen Columbia River. Bone-cold, I pound my ski-boot-clad feet alternately on the floor of the helicopter to produce heat in my lower limbs and combat the chills. Then I stop ... Shivering seems more appropriate.

The aircraft sinks below the cloud base and I see the open waters of Lake Revelstoke below. The drama and stress of the flight evaporate as the air becomes smooth and we fly south along the east shore of the lake. The town, with its grey, muddy streets and chimneys smoking under the overcast sky, is a welcome sight. We fly over happily recognizable landmarks that are incongruent with the day. Gerry lands the three of us on the pavement near the emergency room doors.

I step onto the hard level asphalt with my ski boots, feeling weak and wobbly. Dan and Gerry help me into the hospital and transfer my care in the tan-floored hospital corridor to Darrell, a nurse in a light blue uniform. I turn and thank them as they depart. With the curtain drawn around, damp clothes fall to the floor. I put on a backless gown and crawl into bed quaking, then soothing hot packs are placed on top of me by Darrell. The senior nurse slides the curtains wide open and asks, "Is there someone I should call?"

"My wife, Nancy," I say through clattering teeth, my mind struggling to recall our cellphone number. I picture her at the construction site of the new house, only blocks away. The RN across the room at the nursing station dials the phone, connects with Nancy and tells her that I am cold but otherwise fine. I imagine Nancy's stress on the other end of the line.

The nurse cleans a spot on my right arm and starts a cold IV. Then she takes my blood pressure on the same arm, putting pressure on the IV, and she has to stop. With blind arrogance, I question and judge her competence. Nancy arrives, relieved to see that I am physically okay. She pulls the curtain around again so we can talk with more privacy. I tell her everything, but it is impossible to convey what I experienced. I see and feel her concern.

Quaking fingers contact my small blue cellphone keypad as I call my mother, Sylvia. When she answers, emotion overwhelms me; I sputter, staccato through the tears, "Mom, I'm okay, there's been an avalanche. It's ... not good. People have died. I don't know ... how many yet."

"Oh my God, Kenneth. Are you okay?"

"Yeah, physically fine, just ... cold and ... shocky. Mom, I was buried for half an hour. It was a terrible one."

"Son, you need to know that none of this is your fault!"

"I'm not so sure, Mom."

She repeats, "It is not your fault, Ken."

"I have to go ... I'll keep you updated, I have other calls to make. I love you."

"Bye, son, I love you too. You take care of yourself."

Her words comfort me, but I know that it is not that simple. I make another call, this time to Karl Klassen, the executive director of the ACMG guides' association. My conversation with Karl is helpful, his ever-present pragmatism a gift. Unflustered, he thanks me for the information, tells me that I have his support and wishes me well.

Doctor Morrison, a burly man who is the attending physician, comes in past the blue curtain and says, "Although unconfirmed, the word is that there have been eight fatalities in this morning's avalanche."

I flush with grief and anxiety wondering whose groups they are from, fearful that they are all from mine. I don't want any of this to be real. I see my actions from this morning's tragedy in real terms before me, and I don't like what I see.

From the other side of the curtain a tall, slightly round RCMP constable appears with his hat under his arm. He has a trained, detached countenance, and the black flip-top notebook he wields is intimidating as hell to me. His name badge reads "MUNCH" in block letters, white on black. He is interested in knowing as many facts as possible. Through all of the formality, there is a hint of compassion in his demeanour. He says, "This is a routine report that'll be needed by the coroner."

The word "coroner" knocks me off balance again. I think, *This is not me. I am better than this.*

(The following is a DIRECT PASSAGE FROM RCMP REPORT VERBATIM including punctuation and other errors.)[5]

He asks, "Can you tell me all that happened today with regards to the avalanche?"

"This morning I did weather observations. It was calm, wasn't snowing, about one (1) cm. of new snow, the temperature was minus 4 Celsius. We left the chalet around 8:00 a.m. and skied down to Carnes Creek. Then we skied up to. . oh we had a break at what we call Tumbedown Lake. Then After the break, Ruedi, I was following Ruedi with my group. R started skiing up to Trutoria.. That was the name of the peak. I was working behind him. He was working the switchback up. I was just.. My group was in the first traverse and I had already done one kick turn. I was working up and I looked back at my group and everything was okay and then I felt the settlement and I yelled avalanche. I was riding on top trying to kick my skis off. I saw some of the others hit pretty hard. The rest is just my own story.. The others were gone from my consciousness pretty quickly. I was able to kick my skis off and stay upright then the second wave of snow buried me."

"Were you guiding the group?"

"Yeah, the second group. I am an assistant guide. I was following Ruedi because I was training."

"So was Ruedi the head guide?"

"Yes he was the lead guide."

"How many people were in your group?"

"I had seven (7)."

"Was this the first day up with the group?"

"We started on Saturday. So Saturday, Sunday, Monday. . Today was the third day."

"Do the clients undergo any type of avalanche training?"

"Yeah. We spend at least an hour-and-a-half doing avalanche training beacon searches on the first day. It's actually very comprehensive on what to do if one occurs.. How to search, How to use the Veri Vox two thousand (2000)..Individual searches and how to do group searches."

"This involves the use of probes too?"

"Yeah, there is introduction on how to use them.. be very firm and do it in front of the person who is on the final beacon search."

"Can you describe the terrain you and your group were traversing when the avalanche hit?"

"It was a fairly steep slope. .thirty- three (33) degrees or so..Around there where we were. It was a fairly planer slope (continuous pitch) with a bit of a rib on the right facing the slope. Then it rolled out up top."

"How many vertical feet was the slope you were on?"

"Roughly three (3) to four (4) hundred. It was new

terrain for me so I can't be certain. On the higher end of four hundred (400)"

"Which way was it facing?'

"Southwest facing"

"What was the weather like at the time?"

"It had been a light west wind snowing very lightly.. less than a cm an hour. Then as we started crossing, it cleared up. It was actually high visibility. You could see the slope quite well. It was still the same temperature. . Minus four (4), although I was working off the temperature I took at the start of the morning."

"Where on the slope did you start your traverse and what direction?"

"We did a side approach and entered the slope about midway just to minimize the risk from above as much as possible. It's a typical thing to do. We entered the slope as you are facing the slope from left to right."

"Had you and Ruedi discussed the events of the day prior to going out?"

"Yeah, we discussed objectives, The original play was to go to Fronaly. We had a break and he started skiing to Trutoria. I radioed him and confirmed that's where he was going. In many ways I was the assistant guide, I feel I was just following him and less a part of the decision making process."

"Had this been arranged with Ruedi?"

"Yeah, it was the order of the week that I would be following to learn the area."

"Have you received any formal training as a back-country guide?"

"Yeah, I'm a member of the Association of Canadian Mountain Guides and hold an assistant ski guide's certification since 1998. I am also a fully certified alpine guide. The alpine guide is a summer certification and I hold a Canadian Avalanche Association Level two (2) certification."

"All of your certifications are up to date?"

"Yeah, and first aide certification is up to date as well."

"Were there any types of snowpack conditions checks done this morning?"

"We probed the slope while entering onto it, as far as today, that is all that occurred."

"What does the probing consist of?"

"It's a probe test. You test the terrain as you continue into it. In this case, the snowpack was firm enough and well settled enough that I had to use the handle of the ski pole."

"Does this mean that the slope appeared safe?'

"Yeah, from my judgment the slope appeared safe."

"Did you continue probing as you went?"

"Yeah"

"How often?"

"As I was working in I would probe..Take five steps and probe. This continued until I was well into the slope."

"It tis a common or practiced type of test?

"Hm, Hmm"

"Had Ruedi discussed any possible danger to watch out for or did anything seem unusual?"

"No. There were no warnings or communication from him at all. He was just skiing up making the track."

Were there any avalanche warnings in effect that you know of or what was the level?"

We usually just worked on our own observation, but yesterday we checked.. So whatever they published yesterday. I can't remember to give you that right now."

"Were there any indications that a slide might be eminent?"

"No"

"Will you read this statement over? Is there anything you want to change or add?

"The avalanche danger scale from Rogers Pass Yesterday was Moderate for at and below treeline and considerable for the alpine. Ruedi called in yesterday and I overheard on the radio."

"What type of slope was the one you were on?"

"It was in the alpine."

"Do you recall the names or details of any of your group?"

I don't know their addresses and phone numbers but I know their names.. First names from many, yeah."

"Could you give them to me?"

"Yeah. Paula, Kathy, John, Dennis, Vern, Jeff, and Joe."

"Is there anything else you want to change or add?"

"No."

"Is this statement true to the best of your ability?"

"Yes." (But inside I say, *No ... we shouldn't have been there.*)

"Thanks for your statement."

The constable finishes his notes and flips his small pad closed, then disappears outside the curtain.

I try to relax and warm up, but my mind darts and loops, replaying every aspect of the day. I want to change it: change the day, my decisions, change my actions, change my inaction, speak-up, stand-up. I realize that I did not see people behind me on that slope; I only saw objects. Now they are real – human beings with lives they wanted to live. Now it is all too real. I wish I had protected them with the truth I saw and felt. Then

I think about how I can avoid responsibility for any of it – the truth too scary to face, my mind continues to construct defences.

In time, I stop shivering. In an invisible but real bubble of shock and dismay, I get dressed in my clothes that are still slightly damp and Nancy and I make our way out the front of the hospital. I look fine because I am walking and breathing. At one and the same time, it seems a miracle, yet I feel shattered and everything is wrong. Nancy is happy I survived; I feel shame. We drive to the new house in the failing late-afternoon light. When Nancy had received the call from the hospital, she was grouting the stone tile in the entryway of the new house. She had immediately abandoned what she was doing and come to the hospital. The grout is now drying and needs to be trimmed, scraped and wiped from the stone. Although it is a stupid thing to do right now, it cannot wait. Nancy offers to take me to our rental home downtown, but I do not want to be alone.

We arrive at a house that is cold, dark and foreboding. Clicking on the yellow halogen work light illuminates the immediate space, yet darkness looms everywhere else. With the entryway lit, Nancy begins work, scraping and wiping off the red grout with a wet cloth. Unable to find the strength to pick up any task, I sit on the stairs above the entrance, watch and stare through Nancy as she works. My group and I were buried in an avalanche; I know that as many as eight people were killed, but I have no idea who, other than Dave. I feel the shame of catching myself thinking about how this will affect my life, my career and my family. I look at the walls in disbelief. All of our hard work is before my eyes: years of dreaming and planning. How can this now have any meaning in light of what just happened? Being here in this new home should be a celebration; it is not and might never be. My life is forever coloured black. I replay the day's events over in my mind. I don't want to believe any of it because it all means that I am no good.

My stomach burns with worry and my mind races, replaying all of the uncertainties I had before the event, wishing that I could take back the day. I feel nausea well up about the future, thinking, *Will there be charges? Will we lose the house? What will happen to my career? Will I be judged? I know I'll be judged, but how? What will this mean?* I sit there on the steps, my eyes darting about as I think.

Nancy and I converse but our exchange is distant from my reality. She is concerned but happy I lived. I try to be happy but I feel as if the tragedy did not go according to plan. Whenever I imagined a guiding tragedy, I was not on the list of survivors. I never dreamed of having to live with my decisions; I feel betrayed by this reality. Nancy completes her work and we drive through the snowy streets of Revelstoke to the rental house, where I have a shower and crawl into bed. Thankfully, sleep comes to my exhausted spirit.

JANUARY 21, 2003

I awake to the same nightmare. I eat, but food is only for survival and it crosses my palate without any enjoyment. I talk to friends who are supportive, yet they cannot possibly understand what I experienced and how I feel now. Despite trying to be upbeat with them, inside I feel terrible. My isolation is deeper now. The reports in the media all speak of seven fatalities but release no names. I await a call from the chalet that never comes and I feel invisible, as usual. Finally, a call comes in from Ingrid at the SME office. She says, "Hey, Ken, how are you?"

"I'm surviving, but I'm more than a little stressed. I don't know what the outcome was up there beyond the fact that there was an avalanche and there were up to seven fatalities. Do you have any more information, Ingrid?"

"No one has called you from the chalet?"

"No, they haven't."

"Sorry, but I don't have any more information for you, Ken, except to confirm that there were seven people killed. There has been so much going on; Ruedi and Nicoline are still at the lodge. I've been fielding questions from the media but telling them that the names have not been released yet. The next of kin have to be notified before any of us can know."

"Okay."

"Hey, if you're interested in attending, there will be a critical-incident debrief today at the Wintergreen with a counsellor."

"I'll plan to be there. What time?"

"The others are flying out soon and will be there at 1:00 p.m."

Twenty-six hours after the tragedy, I arrive at the Wintergreen Inn to debrief. I walk right past the cameramen and journalists swarming at the front door. They have no clue that I was involved, and leave me alone, but I know they would love to talk to me. I surreptitiously glide by, yet I feel an intense pressure as I walk past, knowing I have something to say but am not brave or coherent enough to say it.

Inside, I see some members of the group for the first time since we were all on La Traviata: Charles, Rick R., Heidi, Rick M., Keith, Bruce and Paula. It is good to see them, but it is a desperately sad occasion. Not all of the guests have come; some stayed up at the lodge to continue skiing. John is giving a statement to the media at the RCMP station while we meet here.

Their faces convey the pain of having seen their friends die. A snow cocoon protected me, and I am completely ignorant about the details of what happened during the rescue; I escaped that trauma. Their expressions tell me that it was hard. Really hard. I know that each one has a story to tell. They are happy that I survived. I feel awkward and uncomfortable with their happiness; I smile, but it feels fake. I am anxious to gather more information: over a day has passed and other than Dave, I have no knowledge about who in our two groups died. I pull Paula aside. Facing her sorrow-filled expression framed by her dark hair, I say, "Paula, I don't know anything. Wha ... who died?" My words are nearly unsayable.

She replies in her French-Canadian accent, "I can't speak their names, Ken. I have to write dem down. Let's go sit."

We sit down side by side on the long couch and Paula begins to cry. With a pencil quaking in her hand, she positions it on the paper and pauses. Cryptically, she writes down the names of the dead slowly, one by one, as if each one needs to be coaxed through all of the emotions. I gently look over her trembling hand. When she finishes, there are seven names:

Dave

Naomi

Craig

Kathy

Vern

Jean-Luc

Dennis

Looking at the hand-pencilled list, I know that life will be different for everyone connected to these people. I also know that my life will never be the same. A black abyss is all around me, a looming fear about myself. It deepens my feelings of inadequacy and validates them. I have proof that I am as bad as I have always believed.

Pain dissipates if I blame others: it is comforting to think none of it is my fault. I sense that there is more, but it is elusive, beyond my grasp. The black abyss looms. Waiting.

The counsellor begins to speak. Her words disappear in the air as my mind processes the interaction with Paula. I fall into my own world: what is going on around me is like a movie playing in the background of my thoughts. I am relieved that not everyone in my group died; that fact matters a lot to me. It matters to me that three were from my group and four from Ruedi's. I witness my competitiveness about these facts with disgust, but it also brings me comfort, as if my lower numbers are a measure of competency.

The circle of people share thoughts and experiences. There is crying, grief and sorrow. I speak but my words are superfluous to my emotions. From my detached trance, I learn about how horrible it was on the surface of the snow during the rescue response. Many communicate feeling inadequate about their effort to help the deceased. I understand, but don't share what I know about my own actions.

The meeting ends. I think about the media out front and envision how they will pepper me with questions when I step out the door. I fear saying the wrong thing or speaking about what I know. The black abyss looms. Abandoning the opportunity, I open a window that leads to the backyard of the inn. I lift myself up to it, squeeze through the opening and jump out into the snowy yard. Like the fugitive I have so often played, I run down the alley and meet up with Nancy, who is waiting in the car where she dropped me off. I get in the car with her and we drive away.

CHAPTER 3

THE ABYSS

JANUARY 23, 2003

Three days following the avalanche is my 38th birthday. We move into our new home on Saturday the 25th with the help of our friends Keith, Lisa, Jeff, Colleen and Brian, who come from Alberta to help us move our things from our rental place into our new home. Nancy suggests we throw what she calls a "Rebirth-day party" while everyone is in town. Strangely, I am keen on the idea. The party doubles as a house warming. Friends from town also attend and I proudly show them all of the exciting features of our new home, as if the house is who I am now. Many treat me like a hero for having survived. I revel in the attention yet it feels artificial, balancing next to the edge of my abyss, the special treatment the only thing keeping me from falling into the place where I feel deep, raw pain. I blow out my birthday candles and lift my arms up in victory. The triumph is shallow because there is no flame inside, my spirit like the stark, smoking stems of the candles I just blew out.

I scare myself with how easily I can pretend to be what I think others want me to be. I have always felt like an actor in my life, playing a role. The dissonance between what I feel inside and what I show to others leaves me feeling more isolated than ever. The truth of my life has drifted further from my grasp.

The opportunity to go to see the families of the victims passes. I write letters instead; screen, keyboard and printer feel safer because I do not have to stand face to face and answer questions that make me examine the event. I also do not have to expose myself to emotion, empathy or compassion – I am too busy marinating in self-pity.

Few blame me. I experience how convenient and comforting participating in a hierarchy can be; I was supposed to follow without questioning. I feel absolved of any responsibility from my peers – most project compassion and say they cannot imagine what I have experienced or must feel like. But absolution does not sit right either. They are right about not being able to imagine. Before this, I had not envisioned this scenario either: being a guide who led people to their death. I always expected martyrdom if a tragic event occurred, and never considered living with the consequences of surviving.

I feel touchy and am hair-trigger sensitive to anything bordering on criticism. Within the first few weeks, another guide asks: "Ken, do you really think you'll ski guide again?" I take his comment to mean that I am banished from the industry. Although I do not confront him directly, the exchange triggers a seething fury that lasts for days and weeks. Unfortunately, Nancy experiences the bulk of my rage, simply because she is there.

I find myself in conversations casting blame on Ruedi. I cannot stop doing this because it feels good, but it is also hollow. There is no shortage of people willing to listen to my tirade and to take sides. In a one-on-one counselling session, the man in the chair opposite says: "Ken, you have no reason to blame yourself for any of this. Everyone knows that Ruedi pushes it, he always has ... that's why people go ski with him. You were just the assistant guide and it was only your job to follow."

FEBRUARY 1, 2003

Twelve days after the avalanche, I go skiing. The invitation to "Get back on the horse" comes from Larry Dolecki, a local guide who has been in Revelstoke for some time. Larry is strong and competent, and I appreciate his invitation. I look up the avalanche forecast for Glacier National Park on the web and read a rating of "Considerable" for the alpine, which causes my gut to flip, but I go anyway.

We choose to ski the moraines of the Bonney Glacier on the west side of Rogers Pass. Our tour begins up the bed of Loop Brook under the domineering snow-laden sides of Ross Peak. I scan the ridgetop as we stride under the behemoth to see the wind transport snow from southwest to northeast high above us. My heart races as I see telltale snow plumes launch off the ridge just visible in front of a grey backdrop of sky. The ski track snakes beside Loop Brook, the water hidden under a thick blanket of snow, but exposed in places. Soon, the route leaves the stream and I relax as we switchback up through the shelter of the massive Engelmann spruce and hemlocks. Our conversation goes to the avalanche. We talk at length and I share what I experienced of Ruedi, the guiding operation and the avalanche. A lot flows out of me, and although the conversation is dramatic, it feels empty because I hide and manipulate details to protect my ego.

We ascend to treeline and I take over the lead and set track in the soft powder snow up the slopes of the terminal moraines of the Bonney Glacier. The light is flat, the white slope only discernible from the sky by the feel of my skis in the snow. I flash back to the avalanche; sounds, images and emotions from the day play, like a looping video, in my head. I hear the snow settle in a massive WHUMMPH!! The screams of "AVALANCHE!" I see dense snow breaking up around me and sliding down the slope. My heart gallops out of control. I take each stride in trepidation, yet put on a good show for Larry. I hold it together and lead us to the moraine crest, where we take off our packs and draw out our Thermoses.

The hot sweet licorice tea warms my insides and calms me. I tell myself, *I can't let on how scared I am.* I take a deep breath and feel safe for the moment, but isolated from Larry.

The distinctive thump of a low-flying Bell 205 segues into my peace. I say to Larry, "That machine is flying low over the Park … it's gotta be from one of the ski operations. Do ya think there's been an accident?"

"Let's radio and find out."

I pull my Kenwood from the top of my pack, screw in the antenna and dial the frequency to the "Glacier Park" channel. I push the button on the side and say, "Dispatch, this is Ken Wylie, I am a guide. Has there been an incident?" There is a long pause, and I nearly repeat my message, when the radio squawks:

"Ken, from Glacier Dispatch: please stand by."

Larry and I wait, in anticipation, facing each other standing ski tip to ski tip, when the radio sparks to life again.

"Ken, from Glacier Dispatch: there has been an avalanche in Connaught Creek with 17 involved. Are you able to assist?"

"Yes. We are two guides, currently at Bonney moraine, en route to Connaught."

"Please report to the rescue staging at Rogers Pass maintenance compound. Keep this channel clear for others calling in."

"Copy: report to rescue staging. Ken out." I keep the radio in my chest pocket turned on to hear the situation unfold.

The new mission evaporates my fear; I see it as an opportunity for redemption. Larry and I strip our skins off our skis and race down the moraine and through the trees. In half an hour the trail deposits us 5 km down from Rogers Pass on the west side, where we load our gear into Larry's little car and drive to the top. At staging, we sign in as active searchers, program the rescue radio frequency into our units, shift our equipment into a running helicopter and fly a short hop up the Connaught drainage to the avalanche site. With a snowy blast, the machine touches down next to a group of teenaged kids, who appear shaken. I climb out of the machine and help them load while Larry goes to the other side to get our skis from the basket. I secure the doors, crouch in the snow beside the front of the machine, confirm that Larry is done with the skis, give the pilot the thumbs-up and he lifts off.

Carrying our skis, we approach the scene, our senses piqued. It is one of massive devastation: a wide swath of avalanche debris fills the valley. The smell of fresh-cut evergreens pervades the air and I see random branches, logs and roots sticking out of the mounded snow. A red and white helicopter hovers over the site with a tower-computer-sized black avalanche transceiver on a tether hanging below. It is searching the deposit for a transceiver signal from a buried victim. A probe line of more than a dozen people stand an arm span apart, facing uphill – this means that they suspect the victim is without a transceiver, either through loss or damage. All of them have an avalanche probe in their hands, their movements synchronized under the direction of a rescue team leader. I recognize that all are from local backcountry or heli-ski operations, because I see uniforms from Selkirk Tangiers Heli Skiing, Canadian Mountain Holidays, Kicking Horse Ski Resort and Selkirk Mountain Experience. We get closer and Abby Watkins, a guide and first responder, appears at the base of the avalanche in her down jacket with a probe in hand, tragedy written on her face. She says: "Ken Wylie, what on earth are you doing here?"

"We were in the area and had to help."

I stick my skis upright in the snow next to some others and Larry and I check in with the site rescue leader, Jordy Shepherd, at the base of the debris. I ask him about the incident and search and he says it is a group of school kids from Alberta, with one person still missing. He tasks Larry with another sweep of the debris and me with the probe line. He reminds us to not pee or spit on the avalanche deposit because it will distract the search dog that is combing the debris with the dog master. We switch our transceivers to receive and continue past skis and rescue equipment, up the debris. I see teenage kids lying in lifeless contortions on the snow, their stiff bodies in the positions they were in when buried. I look at them as though they are a curiosity. I feel nothing for these young people and wonder why, feeling as lifeless as they look. I retreat into my dramatic story and wander around in a daze pretending to be of assistance. I greet other guides I have not seen in a long time happily, and they look at me quizzically. Eventually I join a probe line and follow "three holes per step" commands for thirty minutes. “Forward! Probe right! Probe left! Probe centre! Forward!” probing the snow for the one last missing person, hoping to be the one who gets the probe strike.

The potential for a second slide increases as the wind deposits more snow on the lee slopes above, so the search is called off by the incident commander and nearly a dozen of us pile into a red and white Bell 212 and are airlifted back to staging. Larry and I drive back to Revelstoke. En route Larry says, “Would you have gone there today?” I offer, “We did go to a place like Connaught today.” Larry nods and we say little more on the half-hour ride back to town. Numbness pervades. I am watching rather than participating, devoid of emotion or connection to the humanity of what I am experiencing. I say to Larry as I get out of the car, “This winter Revelstoke feels like a war zone.”

At home, information trickles in and I learn that the kids were from Strathcona Tweedsmuir School in Okotoks, Alberta. Seven of them died. I think about my friend Jim Preston, who works at the school, and I know the disaster that happened at Connaught Creek will affect him deeply, because he is a man who cares.

MARCH 3, 2003

In a daze for over a month now, I work on kitchen cabinet doors in our basement. Shortly after the tragedy, Ruedi tried to convince me to come back to work at Selkirk Mountain Experience. He came over to the house and we sat in the living room discussing guiding. I shook my head in response to his requests to return to work and said very little. I did not tell him why I was not interested in going back up there with him; it just felt good to say no. Instead, I went on employment insurance, uncertain of what I would do for work in the future.

Ironing birch edge-tape onto the plywood cabinet doors for the kitchen, I hear the news that America is going to war with Iraq. The announcement means nothing compared to my own swirling, endless thoughts about La Traviata. I am brooding, angry, scared and shattered, not knowing how to pick up the pieces. I do not want to ski or be with people in the backcountry, but that is who I am supposed to be and what people expect of me. I do not know what else to do. I ask myself, *Who am I now that I have little desire to be in the mountains?* The only answer I hear for myself is: "Nothing." But I also know that can't be true either. Confusion reigns.

While I work on the cabinet doors, I realize that what I fear most is to become one of those broken members of the guiding community that everyone talks about but never engages; a man who gets through his life with a bottle of scotch and a long list of denials. A light comes on when I think about how I want a dialogue with people about the human factors that led to the disaster. I do not know how to do that. I am also afraid. Then it comes to me as a flash: *"To use mountain experiences as an educational tool for myself and for those with whom I travel."*

I had first heard that statement from Bruce Hendricks on the front deck of the Fairy Meadows Hut. He and I were talking about our philosophies and when he shared his statement, it made an impact on me. As I stand in my basement, the words seem to have come straight from the divine. There is purpose – I have come to the surface for a breath.

DECEMBER 2004

My career has moved on and I am working at Thompson Rivers University in Kamloops, British Columbia, in the Adventure Programs department teaching natural history, outdoor leadership, rock climbing, mountaineering and ski touring. The position is demanding, especially while I try to piece back my own confidence amid the predominantly over-confident young men and women who are my students.

Two years is the end of the statute of limitations so I still cannot speak publicly about the avalanche without risk of legal implications, they tell me. However, I feel a need to further process the experience and seek ways to engage my colleagues. Thinking that I need to coalesce the lessons to help myself and potentially others, I approach Curt, an instructor, and float the idea of speaking about the tragedy to avalanche professionals as a sort of internal review. He agrees and we arrange to have me come into a Canadian Avalanche Association Level 2 course he is directing. The idea is to present the La Traviata tragedy as a case study we can all learn from. The Association, known for its cutting-edge avalanche education, is an internationally respected organization.

There are about 20 participants and I address them in a hotel conference room. My talk focuses on the human factors involved in the event, with the main theme being how I abandoned my better judgment. I speak about the problems of hierarchies while working in hazardous environments; how one person cannot read a situation as clearly as a team can. It is an idea I learned from my friend Brian Spear, which he articulated as "hierarchies lead to chaos but they are the only way out of chaos." I share some difficult things, yet I still feel I am teetering on the edge of an abyss, afraid to engage my heart in the matter. But I feel like "having the guts" to stand in front of the men and women and share my experience is somehow bringing me social capital, rescuing me from the abyss.

From his seat at the back of the large fluorescent-lit conference room, one of my colleagues, Perry, asks the question that stops me in my tracks. The question is harsh but honest. He says, "Ken, that season was a strange one. I was monitoring the November rain event and the significant ice crust that it produced. As the season's snow accumulated it was obvious to me that it was a problem snowpack and that I would have to be careful all season. Given what we knew about the snowpack, why did you go there?"

The question rips me to my core. I suddenly feel incredibly alone standing there, undressed in front of my peers and industry apprentices, with everyone waiting for an answer. I shrug pathetically. The answer to the question is well beyond my grasp, so I trip over the words: "I don't know."

I sputter on quickly with my presentation to cover the humiliating gap. My pain shifts to anger and hate as I focus solely on the rationalization that Perry was going for the jugular with me up there, just so he could look good in front of his students. The educational value of his question is valid, but I am not ready to see it that way, so I surround myself with blackness again.

APRIL 2007

My work with the Adventure Programs department at the university is overwhelming, mostly because I cannot say no to people. The pressure the students exert on me is formidable: many want to take big risks but are oblivious of the consequences, deluded by the freedom of ignorance. I see their joy and feel like the one who is the bummer in class because I can't share it with them. My experience with death is something most of my students either do not want to consider, or cannot. After four-and-a-half years of trying to make a difference, I resign. I take work in Revelstoke at the Canadian

Avalanche Association, which has recruited me to develop an on-line animated professional avalanche rescue training tool. It is a high-profile government-funded project, but soon I see that I have made a choice to work for a project leader who is disrespectful and demands more than I can give. I wonder why I continually allow people like this into my life.

FEBRUARY 3, 2008

Completely overwhelmed and in distress, battling seemingly every facet of my life, I fall into my abyss once more, telling Nancy I need a break from it all. I ask if I can use her family's vacation house in Maine for three months to write and reflect. At the end of her rope too, she sets it all up for me before I jump in my Volkswagen Jetta with a duffle bag full of clothes, my wallet, passport and computer, leaving everyone and everything in Revelstoke high and dry.

As the car accelerates up the hill heading east out of town, my eyes flood with tears. I have cried over the last few years, but this time the beads running down my face are ones of authentic pain instead of self-pity.

I make a stop in Canmore at Keith Haberl's house. He and I have climbed together for years and when I arrive at his home, I find him on his driveway shovelling snow. I pull the car up on the concrete pad he has just scraped clean, roll down the window and say, "Hi, Keith. I can't stay long, I'm going on a walkabout."

“Cool.”

“Do you have a copy of Thoreau?”

“I’ll be right back.”

When he returns he has a copy of *The Thoreau Reader* in his gloved hand. He passes it to me with a look of understanding on his face and asks no questions. I say thanks and drive away.

I spend the rest of the entire day weeping until I pull over for the night just east of Brooks, Alberta. The second day I sob all the way to Brandon, Manitoba. Then I cry again off and on during the long trek to Thunder Bay, Ontario. I reach Sudbury on the fourth day, having only cried a couple of times. On day five, I make it to Vermont. Finally, day six is a tearless day that takes me to Nancy’s family’s vacation house in Rockland, Maine. It has been a cathartic drive; five years after the tragedy, I grieve the loss of Dennis, Kathy, Vern, Craig, Dave, Naomi and Jean-Luc at last. Through that grief, I finally learn their names and consider the loss their deaths constituted for their families. And I am also now able to honestly lament my broken heart – the mountains, a place I loved, have become a source of pain for us all. But that outpouring of grief offers a glimpse of the possibility of restoring some balance in my life as well – as if some small part of me is still alive, rather than everything inside me being suspended in a lifeless and deathless torpor.

The house in Maine is on the shore of Penobscot Bay and has all of the creature comforts I could possibly imagine. It is large and quiet with tall windows that look out on the water. I spend my days writing and reflecting during long walks out to the breakwater at Rockland. There is total silence here, and I keep it that way, making an effort to finally hear myself. Tears flow and among several writing pieces, I produce a story about a ski outing during Christmas in 1972. *Cross Country Skier* magazine accepts the story for publication. Writing is allowing latent parts of me to come to the fore; I am able to "feel" for the first time in a long time. While I'm able to rediscover some joy, I remain overwhelmed by a lifetime of residual pain and anger.

Each day I rebuild vestiges of feeling in my life by listening to my heart, but remain afraid of the future – going back to a life of being dominated by others is what distresses me most. So in my mind I begin cutting ties with people who I believe have been trying to control me. Seeking a fresh start, I engage a wrecking ball and take swings at my life, believing I have to begin with those that are outside of myself.

CHAPTER 4

BATTLE WITH DECEPTION

FEBRUARY 20, 2008

I deepen an email correspondence with Shelly, a woman from Calgary I had met while working on the avalanche project with the Canadian Avalanche Association. At the same time I distance myself from Nancy. My communications with her become so brief and stunted that on March 4, by phone, Nancy asks the question: "Are you leaving me?" I reply, "I am not going to lie to you anymore, Nancy." She weeps on the other end of the line. My new-found voice feels harsh and mean, but I do not know how to be anything else right now. I am tired of pretending to be something I am not in order to gain the approval of others. There follow many more pain-filled days on the phone that result in a growing anger in both of us.

No longer part of Nancy's family, I have to leave the house in Maine and drive back to Calgary. On the long journey to the Bow Valley, I send out an email that informs people that Nancy and I have split. I write, "I am leaving Nancy so that I can become the man I have always dreamed of being." The list of recipients is long: among them Karen Michelsen, a beautiful woman with brown eyes and long dark hair who has been in my subconscious since I worked with her at Outward Bound 20 years ago.

There is a brief response from her which indicates support but nothing more. Desperate, I seek connection, looking outward to fill the empty hole inside me. I arrive back in Calgary and find refuge with my sister Shauna's lovely family. The days there become golden memories, sharing life with her, her three teenage kids and the dogs. In the background, Nancy and I battle over the house and our finances while my savings dwindle.

Shelly sends me an invitation to go to her house for dinner. I arrive to find her husband away, but I enjoy a nice meal with her young family. When I leave, she joins me outside and gives me a much-too-long hug; the attention feels misplaced but familiar and exciting all at once. The relationship traverses into emotional territory the next day in her office. She is extremely forward and I participate, revelling in the risk, hoping to find true love. The sex is incredibly fun and dangerous, but I see my effort to become a more open and honest person crumble. When I introduce Shelly to my mom and sister, who know she is married, they surprise me with their acceptance.

In April, I house-sit for Jeff and Colleen in Calgary while they are in Europe for six weeks. I set up a space to write in their dining room and craft a story about the avalanche. My efforts are a battle and the writing is full of anger, but it feels good to fight back at something. I patch more house-sitting gigs together while I await a financial settlement with Nancy.

September comes and I make ends meet teaching one course at Mount Royal University in the ecotourism program. The experience reminds me of my deep worth instructing outdoor programs; I have the first sense in months that my career is not over. Feeling this burst of enthusiasm for my vocation, I start a new job with Outward Bound Canada. But once I start working there I can't help but recognize that I still lead a secret double life: unable to share myself with others authentically, I cannot pass on my knowledge effectively.

Shelly showers me with opiate attention when we are together that always produces a significant high but ends in a dire crash with equal predictability. When I'm alone, I feel relationship pain like never before. It begins to dawn on me that by being a secret lover, I have chosen to live in excluded circumstances where I have no voice in the situations at hand. I begin to spend most nights curled up in a ball, wondering why life has to be so hard. My whole existence is now on Shelly's schedule – she decides where to meet and for how long. At Ghost Lake I wait for her for two hours before she shows up. When I confront her tardiness she reacts with a tantrum.

JULY 2008

Everything feels out of control in my life again and I need to be with the wise to gain perspective, so I fly to Peru in search of answers. I sense I am following others on this path, but I don't care in my hope to gather solutions. The aircraft lands at Iquitos in the heart of the Amazon and I take a motorbike rickshaw to Espiritu de Anaconda. The retreat centre has inviting walkways that link thatch-roofed buildings nestled under the nurturing protection of the Amazon jungle canopy.

The energy of the place and its people is enchanting and I feel my out-of-control spin stop and stabilize. Many important conversations happen with individuals from all over the world who have come here to heal their various traumas. I feel heard through the act of doing something that resonates from deep inside. There is wisdom here. It is different from anything I have ever experienced, in that it feels foreign but also evokes a deep sense of belonging.

We eat a special vegetarian diet, and on the second evening drink a tea that purges by inducing us to vomit. Given the tea and a blue bucket, we wander the jungle until we puke. Both the diet and the purification are in preparation for an ayahuasca journey, a daunting psychedelic sojourn that is in no way recreational.

Ayahuasca is a traditional shamanic brew that combines the qualities of two plants from the Amazon rain forest. The stuff tastes smoky, bitter and a little bit slimy. One plant contains a drug called dimethyltryptamine (DMT), while the other has an ingredient that allows the DMT to safely travel in the intestinal tract and not be denatured by stomach acid. The effect about half an hour after drinking this potion is a waking psychedelic dream that purifies the body and spirit through the exit of negative energy. We have a bucket to throw up in, an outhouse nearby and a shaman, because it is common for people's demons to vacate quite physically during the experience. The shaman offers a space for protection during the vulnerable journey. We are encouraged to ask questions of "Mother Ayahuasca" during our experience, and I ponder mine in preparation for what is for me a terrifying prospect.

It is night four and the first of the journeys when I swill the smoky, slimy brew and lie back on my mat, transfixed about where this voyage might take me. Looking up at the stars through the canopy, I feel the tropical forest flow through my body, a fervent sense of connection where I perceive no separation between me and the jungle that surrounds my body. The sounds from the rainforest seem to originate from inside; the air flows out of the trees and into my lungs and vice versa in a constant exchange of oneness.

I feel a presence, and with trepidation I ask, "Is my relationship with Shelly a good thing?" A female voice responds from the back left part of my head, saying in a clear, articulate voice, "It is very dangerous."

Fear abates after the message and I lie in a state of bliss, feeling an ardent surge of life through my body supported by compassionate beings that surround me. I have a deep sense of healing and in the morning take some wobbly steps, wondering if the voice I heard was my own.

I arrive home and the puzzle piece that has been my life fits neatly back into the drama of powerlessness it was in before I left. In time, I gather the courage to end the relationship with Shelly. Her reaction is explosive: she wails in pain, sends guilt-riddled emails, shows up where I like to run – eventually my resolve crumbles.

JANUARY 8, 2009
I battle on and take another intensive retreat, this time to Yashodhara Ashram in British Columbia for the three-month yoga development course. En route I stop in Revelstoke and see my lawyer to sign the separation agreement from my marriage to Nancy. After reviewing the document, I react as if I have received the short end of the stick, like the youngest of seven children might, unable to control my rage and emotions. My lawyer advises me not to sign it, but after a day of deliberation, I see that going to court will cost more in legal fees. I want the scrap to be over, my life to be different, so I sign the document and the long conflict over "stuff" is complete.

I continue driving south from Revelstoke to the

ashram near Nelson and arrive in time for lunch. I sit down with my bowl of soup at the table; the peace of the place surrounds me and I feel a potential for life so profound that I weep into my meal. In the afternoon, I settle in for the three-month journey into myself.

Shelly cannot leave me alone at the ashram and my peace becomes punctuated. She emails constantly and wants to Skype and talk on the phone. I tell her I am supposed to cut home communications, but she will not accept that, calling me selfish and insensitive.

APRIL 2009

It is early April and I return home to work and to our agonizing personal relationship. Shelly and I bounce in and out of our association and the months clock by. I want a normal, open relationship; she strings me along, saying she will tell her family soon. Summer comes and the situation gets out of hand when Shelly announces that she has breast cancer, which I believe has been caused by stress. It is a terrible thing for her, and suffering proliferates in our lives. I believe the cancer will help her be honest with her family about what is going on with us. She struggles with telling her kids that the family will break up. Excluded from knowing what is happening at the hospital and during much of her treatment, I respond by telling her she is hurting everyone around her by not being honest. She has a fit of rage, screaming and wailing at me. The assault shows that I need stability and it must come from me standing on my own two feet. I make my decision to break off all associations with her.

DECEMBER 2009

I buy a house in the town of Cochrane, northwest of Calgary. Life for Shelly gets complicated when her husband, having found out about the affair, requests she leave home. She has cancer, is bald from chemo and has no place to go. I am consumed by guilt, thinking she will need a place to live after leaving her husband, so I tell her she can use my house while I live with my sister. My intent is platonic, yet I feel like I will not be able to uphold that ideal because of her pressure for us to be a couple. Inside I reel with indecision so I ask for help in deciding what to do. My friend Julian sorts me out by saying, "Ken, I see no good coming from this situation ... it will be a nightmare for you." I listen to him.

I begin to discover through all this trauma that being able to disappoint people to be true to myself is something I need to continue to work on in my life. At the start of my relationship with Shelly I could not say no to her advances. I was enamoured of the attention and blind to the consequences. Now, at the end of it, I see our relationship as a replay of La Traviata – only this time the devastation caused is the break-up of a family. Shelly's metaphor for those days is that they were "the perfect storm," in which several elements converged from different places to create a catastrophe. But this time I feel I am answerable for the role I took among all the players. I hold myself to account by resolving to finally learn something from calamity.

CHAPTER 5

LESSON ONE: ACCEPTANCE

The realization that my experience with Shelly is a repeat of the dubious choices I made leading up to the avalanche in 2003 leads me to wonder how much of my life has been so repetitive. What other mistakes do I keep making over and over until they become well practised enough to be unconscious and comfortable?

In an attempt to help me answer that question, my friend and colleague Brian Spear shared a metaphor used in the hang-gliding world, a community where lessons are best learned before dire consequences manifest: flying a hang glider offers fewer second chances. It consists of an analogy about turning life events into gained experience and wisdom.

"There are two jars in any one person's life. One jar is full of marbles, each glass sphere representing an event that will happen in one's life. The other jar is empty, a place reserved for experience and wisdom gained. When we live through an event, it is as if we take a marble out of the first jar and hold it between our fingers. If we ponder what the event means and what positive lessons we can honestly and transparently learn from it, and internalize them, we can put the marble into the second jar and bank some experience and wisdom. The process requires putting ego aside and cultivating humility so that the thoughtful reflection on the event takes root. The aim is to empty the event jar and fill the experience and wisdom jar by the end of our lives in equal measure. If we do not take the time to ponder the important positive meaning of the event, in quiet and solitude, we effectively throw the marble over our shoulder and it is gone – the lesson and meaningful experience is lost to us."

I feel like my event jar, in my forties, is below the middle mark, while my experience and wisdom jar is nearly empty.

Oscar Wilde wrote, "With age comes wisdom, but sometimes age comes alone."[6] I first heard the quote from Marc Piché on my full Alpine Guide exam. He recited it to me when he witnessed me setting a poor anchor on the northwest ridge of Mount Sir Donald. I was in a hurry trying to keep up with the examiner and the other candidate, who were on the ridge ahead of us. The message to me was "be diligent." The event with Marc happened before the avalanche tragedy; I threw a marble over my shoulder then that could have been helpful in avoiding the tragedy that was La Traviata.

My love of adventure was inspired by my maternal grandfather. He was a blue-eyed, angular-jawed farmer and CN railway worker named John Grywacheski. As a Polish farm boy in Saskatchewan, he never went to school, so he did not learn how to read or write in English. He read Polish, but that was not much use to him in Canada. Nevertheless, he had both a keen intellect and a gentle wisdom. My mom tells a story from her early days on the farm which best describes his attributes: One day after lighting his pipe from a large matchbox, my grandpa fumbled the carton and it fell to the kitchen floor. The matches scattered all over the linoleum. He was a man who always wanted to engage people in any situation, so he asked my six-year-old mom, little Sylvia, to help him pick them up. As she gathered the matches, she decided to keep a few hidden in the palm of her hand. Several hours later she snuck out behind the barn and mimicked striking the matches on a stone, as she had often seen her dad do while lighting his pipe. Eventually one ignited. Startled by the flash, she dropped the match into the straw between her feet. The tiny flame quickly doubled and tripled in size. Terrified, and with no understanding of how to respond, she fled the scene and went inside the house, telling her mom, Elsie, that she was tired and wanted to sleep. Elsie, baffled by this request because it was late morning, went outside to get water from the rain barrel to wash my mom's dirty feet before she slipped them into bed. En route to the rain barrel, Elsie smelled smoke and gasped in horror once she saw the burning barn.

She and John leapt into action, Elsie feverishly hauling water up from the well to fill five-gallon tin buckets as John cleared the horses from the barn. Then the two of them shuttled bucket after bucket between the well and the barn to douse the blaze. In time they put out the fire, but not before scorching flames had devoured the east wall of the barn.

Back inside the house, Sylvia cowered in fear under the kitchen table. Eventually an exhausted John walked slowly back into the house, knelt down gently, took hold of his little girl's left ankle and carefully pulled her out from under the table. Once she was beside him, he said softly, "Now you know not to play with matches."

Sylvia escaped punishment; her father did not yell at or spank her. I think John wisely understood that the situation was punishment enough and that any chastisement might break Sylvia's spirit, destroy her curiosity or become the focus of the event, instead of the intended lesson.

My experience of my grandfather was one of acceptance. He also wanted to teach me about reflection, or at least that is how I like to think of it now. He said nothing but he modelled a way of being through fishing. We did this at Madge Lake, near the Manitoba boundary, where my grandparents owned a cabin. Sometimes I went alone with him, other times with my brothers, sisters or cousins. Grandpa had a flat-bottomed aluminum boat we would launch at the dock at Madge. It was as if for my grandfather, the whole process of fishing, when I look at it now from my adult perspective, was a meditation. He made decisions methodically. Typically, we kids never had the patience to wait for the perfect day to fish, but he never compromised his assessment of the conditions under our pressure. If the lake was choppy, we did not fish. Sometimes he did not verbalize a reason for staying off the water, which I now know was wise; he was probably relying on his intuition.

When we did go, he always prepped the boat well before the journey. He kept the motor maintained, the boat lake-worthy, oars aboard and the frog box full. At the water's edge, he parked the gas can on the floor, placed the rods on top of the aluminum bench seating and stowed his green metal tackle box in the back. Once we were in our flash orange keyhole life jackets, he instructed us how to clamber into the boat and sit squarely on the benches. I can see him now, with his pipe tightly clenched in his teeth, draw out the choke knob and pull the starter cord a few times until his green four-horsepower motor came sputtering to life. After adjusting the idle, he would look to a distant landmark and turn the throttle in his hand to get the boat to gently gain speed.

Sometimes he adjusted the motor to putt-putt along at quarter throttle and we trolled with spinning lures. Other times we motored across the lake at full throttle until we found a quiet spot to position ourselves at what Grandpa would announce, in his thick Polish accent, as "the goot place."

Once anchored, with strong, tanned hands he would demonstrate preparing the rods. He'd put red and white floats on our fishing lines, deftly tie on a hook, add lead weights, select a live frog from the box and then, with his firm grasp, delicately pierce the barbed hook through the soft white skin under the chin and up through the firm top lip of the squirming little frog. If we were up to it, we did it all ourselves. It seemed cruel, but he mastered respect for all creatures while doing a required task.

Grandpa was good at casting: he could send a frog and float spinning off into a calm, fish-laden part of the lake. We kids tried, but with varying degrees of success. He always untangled our lines without a word or hint of frustration if we screwed up. That was what was most amazing about him – his ability to cultivate our relationship through patience and acceptance. Once all of our floats were in the water, we waited and watched. It was then that I developed a reverence for quiet.

As I sat in the boat, nature unfolded before my senses. I smelled the decaying cattails and reeds in the marsh at the edge of the lake. I saw a beaver swimming with the trademark V behind as it made its way from the shore with a stick for its lodge. I heard the sound of a red-winged blackbird, roosting on the water's edge, with its distinctive *ok-kaa-leee* song. I felt the warm sunlight that filtered through the leafy birch trees on shore and onto the surface of the water.

Such stillness drew me into being there fully and completely; moments turned to hours and we were all enthralled, waiting for a red and white float to disappear. The only human sounds were from Grandpa whacking his pipe onto the palm of his hand to empty the ashes and soot before reloading it with fresh tobacco, and the click and strike of his chrome lighter.

Stillness invited self-knowledge: fishing was the activity, but knowing ourselves better might very well have been the goal. At first I was a little uneasy with silence, but gradually I began to recognize that my grandpa was comfortable in quiet. I came to understand it to be part of his strength, and therefore something to emulate. To be comfortable with stillness now means to know I am at peace within myself.

As an adult I had mostly forgotten about my grandpa's formative influence on my life, until a woman psychic in Revelstoke, whom I saw when I was there to sign the separation agreement in January of 2009, brought him back to me by saying, "I can see an old man with silver hair, a hat and a pipe standing behind you. He's watching out for you." Hearing her say those words sent shivers down my spine. Since then, his presence in my life has remained constant.

My experiences with my grandfather taught me to love and respect nature, and that it was up to me to find the positive lessons in my experiences. I had lost this lesson for most of my adult life. I'd thrown the fishing marble over my shoulder into the cattail marsh at Madge Lake, below the beaver dam. Now, writing about Grandpa John, I retrieve it and place it in the second jar.

My father, on the other hand, set an example for living that could not have been more different from Grandpa John's. Like my mother, I was curious, and in the spring of 1972 I let my passion for adventure lead me down a similar path to hers – finding my way in the world by exploring it head on.

On that April day, the lunch buzzer sounded at St. Thomas Aquinas School in southwest Calgary. A throng of Grade 2 kids streamed out of the classroom and into the cloakroom to don mud season wear. While he pulled on his boots, Darryl Tryhuk asked, "Want me ta show ya a quicker way home?"

With no idea what he had in mind, but intrigued, I said, "Okay." Travelling in the opposite direction from my home on 43rd Street, we walked diagonally across the field, heading northeast, our feet treading on brown grass and half-frozen earth. One at a time, we stepped over the single-cable fence and ambled east down 25th Avenue. The sun warmed the skin on our faces and hands, and melted snow flowed in the street gutters. We passed Glendale Community Centre, nestled in a natural amphitheatre.

My internal clock sensed the lunch hour tick away as

we drifted along aimlessly, but I loved exploring. The community centre basin was home to a rectangle with rounded corners of four-foot-high plywood and two-by-four boards. The rectangle contained only water and mud – the spring remnants of the community hockey rink – smelling like my mom's compost heap.

At the corner of Glenmount Drive and 25th Avenue, Darryl pointed to something that had caught his eye, saying, "Look at that." It looked like a red toy house with a gabled top. In white lettering, the word FIRE stretched boldly across the front of this inverted toaster-sized box. Darryl said, "How 'bout if you pull it?" Keen to find out what would happen, yet sensing but ignoring that it might not be a great idea, I clambered up the stand with Darryl's assistance. As I balanced on his cupped hands and against the crimson post, my arm extended, I flipped open the white Pop-Tart-sized hatch and pulled down the hook with the outer fingers of my right hand. My mission accomplished, I lowered myself back down to the sidewalk with Darryl's help.

The next moment, we heard the distant, urgent sound of the fire-engine siren originating from Station Eight, the fire hall I had visited in kindergarten. Suddenly the gravity of the situation gripped me; my mind's eye pictured the blood-red fire truck streaking to our location. We gaped at each other in horror for a split second before we shot off like a couple of champagne corks, sprinting along the streets, crossing 26th Avenue, skittering around corners and, finally, ducking into the alley between 41st and 40th streets.

The siren fell silent as the fire truck reached the red alarm box. It took them only a moment to realize the prank; nobody was at the post to meet them and there was no sign of fire, smoke or other emergency. From blocks away, we knew whenever the driver put his foot on the accelerator; the throaty rumble of the massive diesel engine betrayed the truck's location as it crept along the streets, crew alert and scanning, searching for the perpetrators. They circled block after block, drawing nearer, the loop tightening as they closed in on our back lane.

The fire engine appeared in the gap at the end of the alley and almost passed. Curiosity betrayed us again when we poked our heads out from behind several beat-up galvanized garbage cans noxious with the odour of rotting food. The rig reversed and turned into the opening of the lane, its huge tires with their chrome lug nuts rolling onto the gravel. The hiss of the air brakes punctuated our fate as the behemoth came to a stop before us. Realizing that we'd been seen, we stepped out from behind the cans and tried to play it cool. Side by side we walked up to the engine, hands in our pockets, as Darryl whispered, "Just pretend we're headed back ta school."

A dark, angular, mustachioed man in a navy-blue uniform clambered down the gleaming pump truck. Striding up to us in his polished black boots on that sunny spring afternoon, he called out, "Hey, boys, how are ya?"

"Fine," we said, grinning in an effort to contain our anxiety.

Then he added, "Can I see your hands?"

The question seemed non-threatening, so from blue denim pockets we produced our hands. At the sight of the green paint on them, the horror of the truth swept over us both. The fireman said, "Yup, the alarm had paint on it." The dye had been on the handle of the alarm and had transferred to my hands when I pulled the hook. Darryl's hands must have picked it up as I came down from his boost. Without a doubt, I was the one who had done the deed, and to my left was my accomplice.

From his breast pocket, the fireman produced a black flip-top notepad and asked for our names, phone numbers and addresses. Mortified, I gave him my information, imagining prison life as I spoke. In turn, he took Darryl's information.

After his pen stopped moving, he closed his notebook and said, "Did you know that pulling an alarm is a serious offence?"

Kicking the grey gravel at our feet, we each mustered a pathetic "no."

"It's serious because we're no longer available if a real emergency happens. It means that if someone really needed us they'd have to wait; that time might be the difference between life and death for them. We'll have to escort you home so your parents know what you've done."

My pulse thumped in my dry throat.

The fireman keyed the microphone clipped to his lapel: "Dispatch, this is Eight Pump."

"Eight Pump, go ahead."

"We have a couple of boys who pulled the alarm at Glenmount Drive and 25th. We'll escort these young gentlemen home but I need you to put a call in to each of their parents to make sure someone's at the residence when we arrive."

"Go ahead with the names and phone numbers."

"Boy number one's first name is Kilo, Echo, November, November, Yankee. Second name: Whiskey, Yankee, Lima, India, Echo. At 242–2619."

"Copy: Kenny Wylie, 242–2619."

"Affirmative."

"Boy number two's first name: Delta, Alpha, Romeo, Romeo, Yankee, Lima. Second name: Tango, Romeo, Yankee, Hotel, Uniform, Kilo. At 249–6045."

"Copy: Darryl Tryhuk, 249–6045."

"Affirmative."

"I'll put those calls in. Dispatch out."

"Eight Pump out."

The fireman led us to the door of the candy apple truck and we ascended the steps and the chrome railing into the back compartment of the engine. A mix of emotions welled up inside me while I sat amidst the well-tuned equipment and the men.

The fireman calculated with the driver that Darryl's home was closer, so it would be our first stop. The engine operator manipulated the large-diameter steering wheel before him, guiding the vehicle down the alley to the pavement and onto 42nd Street and the duplex where the Tryhuks lived.

As the truck idled in front of Darryl's house, I clearly saw the process of reality unfold. The crisply dressed fireman led Darryl right to his front door, rang the bell and spoke with his mother, whom I could see from a distance was both respectful and angry. In a few minutes, he returned to the engine, scaled the railing, came through the door and sat down beside me. My house was next.

As we bounced along, I said to the fireman, "Can you drop me off a block from home? I think I've learned my lesson."

Projecting his voice above the noise of the vehicle, he said with a broad smile, "No, I think it's best that we speak to your mom." Then he asked, "Why did you pull the alarm?"

"I dunno," I said with a shrug.

The engine pulled up in front of my brown stucco house on 43rd Street. We climbed down and walked across the pavement, along the walkway and up the three concrete steps to the front door. The fireman rang the doorbell and my dad, expecting the visit, opened the door and looked beyond us to the massive red engine, then glowered down at me. I had prepared myself for my mother to answer the door.

While Mom talked to the fireman, Dad led me roughly by the arm to the bathroom, lifting me to my toes as we walked. Furious, he scrubbed at the indelible green paint on my hands with a fingernail brush and soap. My skin turned red and the pigment faded little. He seethed, "Good boys do not pull fire alarms!!! Since you can't be a good boy in my house, I'll have to throw you out on the street!!!"

I wept while I conjured up pictures of suddenly being homeless, fending for myself. After trying to get the paint off, my father left me to sit on the hardwood floor in the hallway, next to the bathroom, to cry and wonder when my homeless life would begin.

I remember distinctly that I had mostly caught on to the fact that needing Darryl's acceptance and approval was why I had pulled the alarm. I had identified it in a flash when asked by the fireman, but like most kids I couldn't admit it and so decided to say "I dunno."

My father's reaction deepened the problem: threatening me with homelessness reinforced my fear of being shunned, keeping me in the prison of doing things motivated by my need for the acceptance of others and not for myself. Dad had always worried about what others might think. Perhaps he was concerned about one of his seven kids becoming delinquent and bringing shame upon the family. I know he worried about the community accepting our family; his change of our ancestral name from Werbowski to Wylie helped us fit into the community on the surface, but on another level we remained stowaways. So we had the benefits of getting where we wanted to go on the social ladder, but at the cost of knowing and standing in our truth.

My father believed in "deny thy self" – he cultivated the habit of always sacrificing his needs for what he thought others desired of him. So he gave of himself what he could not afford, and that fuelled his resentment: loved in the community, at home he had a fiery temper that uncorked in an instant. I learned that pattern well because over the years I always hoped that if I did what others wanted me to do, I would reap their love in return. When this did not happen, I got angry and bitter – like my father.

My need to be accepted by others underpinned most of my choices after that fire alarm misadventure. It became impossible for me to say no to people when they asked things of me, for fear of judgment or exclusion. Eventually I even had a hard time holding down a job, because failing to say no, to protect myself, always led to burnout. Over the years I have agreed to nearly impossible situations that were desperate for me to live with. My first years at Thompson Rivers University after the avalanche are a good example: I agreed to live alone in a basement apartment in Kamloops and commute home two hours to Nancy in Revelstoke on weekends. At the time it was the worst thing I could have done for myself – I was trying to heal and needed support. Instead, taking that job in what I thought was a sacrifice for my family merely led to more bitterness and anger, for me and everyone else.

La Traviata is a repeat of the fire alarm story. My first stride onto the slope after standing at the edge was motivated more by a need for acceptance from Ruedi than by acknowledging and accepting my own truth, and keeping me and my clients safe regardless of what I thought anyone was asking of me. I failed to follow my own inner compass and, in so doing, abandoned my responsibility. My desperate need for external validation clouded the realities and what would become the devastating consequences to my guests and their families. In seeking the acceptance of others, I have always achieved the opposite. Trusting that I am good enough just as I am will keep me from giving "gifts" I cannot afford. Making good decisions requires self-acceptance first.

In writing this story about my father, I remember most of all my initial flash awareness of the true answer to the fireman's question. I retrieve a red marble from inside the fire truck and place it in the second jar.

CHAPTER 6

LESSON TWO: COURAGE

FEBRUARY 24, 1978

When I was thirteen, my family went to Lake Louise to ski and to watch the downhill race at the Shell Cup Canadian Championships. It was a beautiful, clear, blue-sky winter day in Banff National Park. The snow-laden peaks surrounding the Lake Louise ski area sparkled in the sunshine. A festive air pervaded the resort, with Shell Cup banners flying, music playing and announcers keeping the spectators informed about the events and racers' times. It was also a day that now punctuates my understanding about the meaning and scope of courage.

My father was a gate official for the race. His job was to make sure the competitors skied on the correct side of each blue and red plastic gate marking the line of the course. I was there to watch and to ski the nearby slopes. Feeling the cool mountain air on my body, I rode up the chairlift and drank in the excitement of the event. From this lofty seat, I could get an overall view as the Lycra-clad, helmeted racers careened down the sinuous, ice-hard line. I had never before seen skiers reach velocities of 145 kilometres per hour. I watched in awe as they hurtled past me, powerfully displacing air without any noise from a motor. I pictured myself in their situation and felt the call. In my soul, I wanted to know if I possessed the same courage to race at breakneck speed like my heroes did.

Skiing was a miracle come true in my life. Two years earlier, at St. Thomas Aquinas Elementary School, my Grade 5 teacher had passed out information forms for ski lessons at Paskapoo, the local ski hill. Filled with excitement, the form in hand, I walked home hoping with all of my heart that I would be able to participate. To my delight, Mom said, "Some of the older kids have gone – I don't see why you shouldn't go."

We arrived at the ski hill by yellow school bus, all decked out in our winter clothes. Those of us who needed equipment received a set of yellow K2 skis with brass Spademan bindings, as well as plastic boots and a pair of ski poles that bore the tweaked signs of many crashes. After I changed into my boots, my feet skittered on the concrete floor as I made my way to the snowy landscape outside.

It was cold, the hill packed with skiers from other schools preparing for their day. In the background, with a constant jet-like sound, snow guns blasted out hard, man-made snow, a substance not unlike the stuff on the inside wall of a freezer chest. Paskapoo was a white island in a sea of midwinter Calgary brown.

Patience was the key with the Spademan bindings, as they were not of the simple step-in type. They had only a clamp that pinched a plate mounted below the heel of the boot and required three hands to operate. After succeeding in getting my skis on, I met the rest of the ski school participants in front of the main lodge by a tall wooden sign inscribed and painted "Ski School Meeting Place."

Susan, my instructor, had curly dark hair that was rarely under a hat no matter how cold it was, a big smile and very cool green and white Kazama skis. She was a strong skier and a competent instructor, but most of all she was patient. We started with a tiring series of sidesteps up the concrete-like snow at the bottom of the hill rising up to the front of the day lodge. A short distance up, with all of us in a line facing her, Susan demonstrated a wedge with her skis that she called a "snowplow." "This will slow you down," she said. When my turn came, I pushed the tails of my skis out in a wedge and felt the control it gave me, but not the thrill I sought. I wanted things ramped up. Next, she showed us the snowplow turn and demonstrated shifting her weight to one ski while in a wedge sliding down the hill. Her body went in the direction the weighted ski faced. One at a time each of our group members followed the snaking tracks Susan had made for us in the snow, by shifting our weight from one ski to the other as shown. It was okay, but I wanted to go faster. In time, after more practice, Susan released us for the afternoon, saying, "You guys have the rest of the day to practise on the rope tow. That's a great place to use what you've learned."

I skipped the rope tow on the "bunny hill" and fumbled my way up the T-bar ski lift, past the noise and fog of the jet-like snow guns, to the top of the seemingly massive hill. Standing on the flat, snowy summit, skis underfoot, I marvelled at my position above the brown and grey winter city.

My pole tips squeaked in the snow as I pushed from a standing-still position, until gravity took hold and my ski-supported body began to accelerate. I felt growing air resistance against my winter pants and navy blue K-Way jacket. The bumps on the snow's surface increased in intensity as I gained speed and momentum. Wind whistled in my ears, my eyes watered and my skis clattered, now gaining more speed than I wanted. Without warning, the snow grabbed one of my ski edges and my foot ripped from my left binding. For a moment I was painlessly airborne before I slammed into the rock-hard whiteness. The shock wave travelled through every bone, my head ached and tooth fillings rattled from the impact. My hat, poles and mittens ejected from the centrifugal force. The skis' sharp edges flailed around my body, attached by the "safety straps" around my ankles. After sliding to a stop, I picked myself up and gathered my yard sale items, boots skittering on the icy slope, and I wrestled with the Spademan bindings until I got the skis on again. After mustering my courage, I pointed my skis downhill in a figure eleven once more only to repeat the same calamity.

At the bottom, I arrived bruised, battered and weary after four rattling falls, having wrestled my skis back on each time. Gliding safely to a stop where the slope turned level, I reflected on my first run. I thought, *Geez, that was scary. Next run, I'll have to snowplow and turn.* Applying the skills I learned from Susan on my second run down was a resounding success.

At the end of the week, Susan called my parents and asked them to come to the hill to speak with her. At the meeting, she told my mother and father that I had potential as a skier and that I should join the Nancy Greene race league. After deliberation, my parents let me ski, so Peggy, Shauna, Mom, Dad and I all became downhill skiers. It was a powerful event in our family that kept my father broke for some time.

Each weekend and several nights during the week, Dad drove me to Paskapoo for practice and competitions. Racing proved to be a great outlet for me at the age of 12. I became a lover of winter, and when not on the hill I spent hours tuning my equipment in the basement. I repaired and waxed my ski bases, sharpened my edges for the ice and kept my bindings lubricated and adjusted. For the first time in my life I did not need reminding to take care of something. The burning passion at the base of my gut motivated all the effort; my hands kept occupied and my mind stayed focused on a dream.

While busy, I pictured the rush of accelerating down the hill as fast as I dared. Speed was my focus – I was not sure what my limit was, but I wanted to find out.

In 1976, after my first year of racing, I won the Most Improved Skier award from the club. I was neither the fastest nor the strongest technically at slalom, a course consisting entirely of turns, many of them extremely tight and close together. My strength resided in boldness and I wanted to compete in the straighter downhill events, but I had to wait until I was 16.

Those years were the golden age of downhill racing in Canada. From 1975 to the early 1980s, Canadian racers, for the first time, competed head to head with racers from Europe on the World Cup circuit. On CBC and other media, I religiously followed the careers of Ken Read, Dave Irwin, Dave Murray and Steve Podborski – whom European coach Serge Lange, after watching their fearless style, dubbed "The Crazy Canucks."[7]

This group consisted of excellent skiers and great men. Watching shows about them on CBC in my youth, I learned that they beat the odds in Europe with teamwork. Each would share information about the racecourse after they had competed their runs in order to help the team get better results at World Cup events. Co-operation was a strategy rarely used by the Europeans, who all competed fiercely, including within their own ranks. In some cases, the tactical tips the Canadians passed on to each other allowed the next team member to eclipse the efforts of those who had already run the course, but the information allowed for a better team result. "The Crazy Canucks," I learned from being glued to every media piece in those days, were "movie star famous"[8] in Europe and slowly becoming household names at home – they inspired me to my core when I was 12 and 13 years old.

But then, on a crystalline day in early 1978 at the Lake Louise ski hill, my father witnessed something that affected my racing future. As a gate official, he tended a portion of the race course just below a component called Double Trouble. At Double Trouble, the athletes negotiated two highly technical transitional jumps. The bumps demanded perfect timing, each requiring a pre-jump – a technique whereby a racer jumps into the air just before the bump and lands slightly after its apex. This strategy neutralized the potentially disruptive effect of the feature by minimizing the racer's time in the air and maximizing his speed and control.

Dad saw a competitor by the name of Scott Finlay crash at this spot. Finlay waited too long to initiate this technique, and as a result launched off the first jump with excessive speed and height. He landed with his weight too far back on the tails of his skis, out of line and control, so the next jump catapulted him into a random cartwheel that slammed him repeatedly into the icy course. Dad's description of what he saw after Finlay hit the ground was, "He was a rag doll, tumbling down the slope."

The images of Scott Finlay's wreck sequence, taken by John Colville, appeared in the *Calgary Herald* newspaper. Scott's and his parents' lives were forever changed. The crash rendered Scott unable to walk or talk from the debilitating head and brain injuries he sustained. He still lives with his aging parents, Hugh and Rosemary, in Napanee, Ontario, today. That Shell Cup misadventure took place 36 years ago.

Witnessing Scott Finlay's fall gave my parents a broader sense of the dangers involved in downhill racing. After careful consideration, they told me I could not race in that discipline. For months afterward I kept the newspaper clipping of Scott's crash in my room; I lay in bed and pondered my own loss while looking at the images. Racing resonated deep inside me and the only reason I was a slalom racer was to build the skills I needed to be able to race in the downhill. I was heartbroken, yet lacked the strength of will to tell my parents what it meant to me. I felt misunderstood and alone, yet still I did not say anything. I had witnessed the brutal clashes with my parents when my older siblings spoke their minds to them; the yelling and drama that resulted was distressing and painful to experience. Abandoning my courage, I decided to keep the peace and not openly communicate my innermost passion. I was more afraid of my parents' reaction than I was of racing the downhill, with all of its associated risks. I lacked the courage to simply say, "Racing the downhill is my dream." The next year, I quit racing.

SEPTEMBER 1985

In a boxy green panel van driven by a man whose craggy face and scarred hands betrayed his many granite encounters, Dave Bartle and I entered Yosemite Valley. Dave was a British expatriate and one of my early climbing partners in Calgary. Ten years older than me, he had thinning blond hair, a trimmed beard and a Scottish accent; a great companion. After rounding the corner on Highway 120 and going through the natural tunnel, I saw "The Valley" for the first time. We had arrived on our pilgrimage.

The instant I saw the view from just past the underground passage, I understood why Yosemite is considered one of the rock-climbing community's Meccas. Before us lay the tapestry that is Yosemite: the sacred elements of earth, air, fire and water entwined to dazzle the eye. Three-thousand-foot glacier-etched-and-polished granite walls guarded all sides of the valley, anchoring its power and strength. Air that lent distant images a blue hue communicated depth and mystery. Light from the fiery sun accented the features of the stone with a rich golden glow. And water flowed everywhere; not only in the meandering Merced River through the valley's bottom, but in the abundant waterfalls that leapt from the massive heights of the quartz, mica and feldspar walls on all sides. Yosemite, like the best art or craft, strikes one as divinely inspired.

Our ride ended at Camp Four, the walk-in campground. I spent the afternoon strolling around the park, my perception opened in ways that did not happen for me in the blinding familiarity of home. The new sights, sounds and smells heightened my awareness. I gaped, head cocked back to miss nothing. The sun felt warm and powerful to my cloistered Canadian skin. I took in the sweet smell of ponderosa and sugar pine needles, the touch of cool shade from the oaks, the taste of granite dust that rose from the trails, the resounding roar of the waterfalls high above and the sight of multi-coloured granite, painted liberally by black, green, orange and grey lichen.

Dave and I climbed rock in this enchanted place, the well-established routes taking us up all different sides of the valley. I felt my body growing stronger during the weeks I was there, my pasty white Canadian skin turned golden and it seemed that the stone itself taught me how to climb both its cracks and its smooth features.

We met other Canadians, among them Geoff Powter and Jan Hodgkinson, who had come down together in Geoff's 1972 Volkswagen van. Some days, when ascending single pitches near the valley floor, we climbed in one large group. On rest days, Geoff liked to spend time in El Cap Meadow sitting on a log in the shade of an oak, next to the Merced River, gazing up at the towering walls. Through a pair of binoculars, he studied climbers who were on multi-day routes up the kilometre-high face of El Cap, a vertical and overhanging wall of granite that is the captain of cliffs in Yosemite. I went with him one day; the experience drew me into a new world of potential. Geoff had been up on the wall on numerous occasions, and as a young climber I had been smitten with the idea of being able to scale this monolithic feature. However, at that time I would have been out of my depth. He suggested that for me an appropriate stepping stone to climbing El Cap would be to ascend Washington's Column.

On our third week, Dave and I attempted the Column. It was our first "big wall" route, which we intended to spend two days climbing. On the second pitch, I chose to climb the left corner instead of the difficult right-hand crack system. With more courage than skill, I launched up the daunting corner crack, which I lay-backed instead of jamming face on. Near the end of the lead, with arms fading, about eighty or a hundred feet up from Dave, I placed a small camming unit blindly behind a flake, assumed it was good without checking, and then trusted it to hold my weight as I lowered, hanging from the rope, using friction with my feet to push myself to the right. My goal was to get to a small ledge where I envisioned anchoring myself to belay Dave up. The cam came flying out of the crack when I was halfway across the traverse.

Instantly weightless, I soared through the air, pulling out a few more of my shoddy pieces of protection on my way down. During that moment of weightlessness, I thought I had made the worst error a climber can make:

a failure to double-back the harness buckle of my simple Whillans diaper-style harness, which could detach me instantly from all of the climbing systems. I fell though the air thinking I was a dead man. On my perceived trip to the other side, a woman with beautiful brown eyes, tanned skin and long dark hair flashed before my mind's eyes. She was reclined, and I was lying next to her. The vision disappeared the instant I reached the end of my rope and realized I had survived. Dangling at the end of the cord over hundreds of feet of air, I looked to the right to see Dave standing on the ledge, holding my lifeline in disbelief. Adrenaline invaded my cells, hands and body trembling; the height of the fall, even though I was attached to the rope, was enough to be mortally wounding, but I had fallen down a clean, blank section of the wall and had been fortunate to hit nothing. All I got was a bruised ego, and a tweaked left thumb from the climbing equipment that clattered down the rope to greet me at its end.

After the fall I needed time to heal physically and psychologically. It seemed right to return to Canada, to go back to work and school in the winter. I packed my backpack, stood by the Chevron gas station on the perimeter of Camp Four, stuck my thumb out and made my way back home. Even though I had taken a big fall, I knew I'd learned from the experience. I left Yosemite with dreams, but this time they were mine alone to follow as I saw fit.

Eleven years later, under the weight of one of two

haul bags filled with food, water and equipment, I walked to the base of an El Cap route called The Shield, on the very cliff that Geoff and I had gazed at during my first visit in 1985. I vaguely remembered picking out the route with Geoff in the meadow so long ago. At the time, I had been a student learning a new language, and the routes he was naming were going by too fast for me to integrate completely into my memory bank. I thought about Geoff as I carefully placed my feet, one after the other, on the pine-needle-covered granite loam. Geoff had published an inspiring article about his own experience on The Shield many years before. The images and the content of the prose were with me as I strode to the base of the imposing wall.

I was with a man who is as good as they come: Eric Malone – kind, open and a great communicator. We had decided to climb the route in midsummer, punctuating our work at Pacific Crest Outward Bound School in the Sierra. By this point in my life, Yosemite and the Sierra Nevada had become like old familiar friends. I had ticked off my to-do list many of the prominent features in The Valley and travelled into the depths of the Sierra with my students at Outward Bound. I was now at home in a landscape that had been so new to me only a decade before. Yet there were still things to accomplish here.

Eric and I joked that we were "making The Shield," a phrase we had picked up from some foreign climbers. The Shield was another step into the parts of the Sierra that were still unknown to me. It has 29 pitches, so we had time for us to grow accustomed to a new reality; our plan was to spend four days and three nights in the vertical world.

Ascending these walls often requires a mix of free-climbing and aid-climbing. As the names suggest, "free" is to climb without using the equipment to gain elevation and to use features on the stone for upward progress; the rope and gear are only there in case of a fall. When "aid" climbing, on the other hand, one can use anchor gear in the cracks to move upward. The route we'd chosen involved free-climbing for the first dozen or so pitches, then mostly aid-climbing during the latter two-thirds, up the tiny seams that are the only weaknesses in the otherwise seamless granite.

One of us led a pitch, and fixed the rope to an anchor for the second person to ascend with jumars (mechanical clamps for climbing a rope). While the second partner ascended the line, he removed any gear the leader had placed. While waiting, the leader hauled up the two bags just ahead of the partner, with the heavy bags clipped in line with each other, white bag above, black below, the strategy being that if the bags got hung up on a rock feature, the second person would be there to free them.

We climbed the Free Blast, which, as the name suggests, is the free-climbing portion of the cliff. It went well, especially considering the friction of our bags on our ascent of the slabby pitches. Heaving up two hundred pounds of food and water is difficult enough when the bags are free-hanging. But the compounding friction of the slab on them meant we had to add our entire weight to the hauling system, plus reef on the rope by hand with everything we were worth to inch the bags up the wall. On The Shield we would repeat that process of lead, follow and haul 29 times.

The typical schedule for The Shield involves climbing ten pitches to Mammoth Terraces and then fixing a succession of four lines to the ground from there. Normally, once back at the base, climbers ascend the lines and haul their bags only four steep pitches to the Terraces. We, on the other hand, had chosen to start up the wall and not go back down to the ground. This required that we haul our bags up the ten low-angle slab pitches as we went. One person's lunacy is another person's challenge.

Eric and I arrived at the sand-covered Mammoth Terraces fatigued and hand-sore. The crux getting there had been hauling the bags up the Half Dollar pitch, where they jammed several times. Yet we continued to climb another pitch above Mammoth, and then Eric encouraged me to lead even one more pitch and fix a rope on it before dark. It was the twelfth pitch for the day and I was not keen on the idea. But Eric was irrepressibly enthusiastic, saying, "It's always good to wake up in the morning and have a line to jumar instead of having to lead."

I feared his judgment but once again could not bring myself to say no; crumbling under the pressure, I agreed and launched off to climb the pitch quickly, to complete it before dark.

The first hundred feet of climbing went well. Then, in failing light, I was required to make some free-climbing moves in my Trango boots. The free-climbing too initially went well, but without any protection and a few more balancing steps up, I encountered a smooth slab. My boots were better for edging than smearing on glacier-polished Yosemite granite. I roiled in a screaming temper tantrum as my feet slipped on the glassy stone, my last piece of equipment in a crack down in the gloom below, promising a long fall if I made a mistake. After each attempt to solve the move, I stepped back down to a small edge where I collected myself. For a better rock climber, this short section of marble-like stone would not have been an issue. Instead, rage had its way with me; I slammed my hands against the rock in frustration and shrieked obscenities at the top of my lungs.

Trying to collect my wits, with my head resting on the granite slab, I asked myself what was happening. "How did I get here?" In a flash, I realized that I had lacked the courage to tell Eric that I was too tired to lead. *I had put myself here*. I had more physical courage than the personal courage required to be able to communicate honestly with Eric. In time, I realized that only I could solve the problem, since there were no cracks for an anchor for me to use to lower myself back down. After regaining my composure and trusting what little friction my boot soles gave, I got up the pitch and to a spot where

I could set an anchor, fixed the rope to it and rappelled down to the ledge. "Wow, you had a tantrum up there!" Eric said, surprised by my fury.

"Sorry, Eric, I was just scared of falling," I said to him – afraid to admit my problem, I thought to myself. Laughing heartily, I felt as if I had gotten away with something.

With headlamps on, we pulled food and equipment out of the haul bag and settled in for the night, weary from the day but happy to eat our allotted Chunky Soup for the main course and a can of peaches for dessert. I felt embarrassed by my display of frustration but said nothing, afraid to delve into a conversation about the real me. Instead, I put on my jolly mask and decided to have fun for the rest of the climb.

The route above led us to the base of the Shield Roof and the climb's flagship section, the Headwall. The Shield Headwall is a perfectly convex mass of granite with only one tiny penny-wide seam that scores its middle. It is 1,500 feet off the valley floor and 97 degrees steep. This incredibly exposed place was a mind-bending new reality for both Eric and me and offered a potentially well-earned step into a bigger game. We looked up at the terrain ahead, and marvelled at the vision of Charlie Porter, who spotted the line from El Cap Meadow in the early 1970s and then climbed it with Gary Bocarde.

Thirty metres below the Roof, Eric was leading. At the first difficult placement, he chose the wrong tool for the task. Reluctant to pull out his hammer and pitons, he fiddled around with some shaky tapered brass nut placements in the leftward-leaning crack. In a nervous voice, he said, "Watch me!"

I quipped, "Watch you what – fall?"

My comment instantly met with Eric ripping out the brass and taking a good, clean, equipment-jangling whip into the abyss. He laughed, Batmanned back up to his last piece of gear and hammered a 5/8-inch angle piton into the crack with an ascending ring like any nail met with a hammer. Then he sailed up to the belay below the Shield Roof, confident and psyched, the fear of falling in this terrain now behind him.

Entry onto the Headwall was via the committing Shield Roof, best described as a 15-foot horizontal journey with 1,500 feet of air below. I dangled on a jungle gym of slings attached to fixed pitons embedded in the roof crack system while Eric pondered his seemingly lonely position in the universe, seeing the rope travel out into space. In time, he followed me up its underside. When we were together again, he laughed and said, shaking his head, "Cutting the haul bags loose there and watching them swing out into space was mind-blowing."

We prepared to bivouac just above the lip of the Roof, on a portable ledge (like a double-wide cot, with six slings that gather to a single point to attach to the wall), and enjoyed water, our usual Chunky Beef soup and the divine can of peaches. Refuelled, we settled into our sleeping bags, still wearing our harnesses and anchored to bolts in the wall, for a night's sleep.

In the morning, we awoke body-sore, with swollen, stinging hands from two days of hard work climbing and reefing on the bags. The worst was the painful damage to our fingernails that peeled back when caught on the granite crystals lining the cracks we continually reached inside. Eric joked about visiting a manicurist and begging for help for his bloated, aluminum-blackened hands.

From our hanging ledge we watched the canyon wake up as a flaxen day dawned. The bright sunlight descending the cliff above until it reached our hanging camp, chasing us out of our sleeping bags with the rise in temperature. Far below, the dark-green forest morphed to paler shades as light infiltrated the deep valley. Morning fog rose off the ground near the Merced River. Swallows celebrated the new day with aerobatics, and across the valley Sentinel Rock's shoulder began to feel the warm sun.

Our morning poops were delicate, care-filled rituals into paper lunch bags, then deposited in a secure PVC tube for transport to a proper facility after our climb. Shitting in a bag standing next to my climbing partner was challenging. Crap that lands in the water of a toilet bowl stinks way less than poop in a bag. A new vulnerability comes from this kind of proximity pooping, and I was somewhat uncomfortable as I faced the day's challenge of leading our climb up penny-width seams.

In another hour, the haul-bag stuffing was complete and our comfortable ledge disassembled. We moaned when, with nothing to stand on, we took our weight on our harness-bruised hips. I resettled myself in the bosun's chair to take the weight off my waist. Eric launched our day by leading the first pitch; feeling refreshed from the night, he smoothly ascended the aesthetic crack that led him skyward. He did this by placing a piece of equipment in the fissure, attaching an aider (foot ladder) to it and then stepping up time after time, clipping the rope to the gear as he climbed.

The pitch ended at three shiny new bolts that penetrated the solid granite at the base of a feature called The Groove. Eric fixed the rope to the bolts and I ascended it while he hauled the bags, which swung in the air slightly behind me. We rejoined at the anchor, where I collected and sorted the climbing hardware in preparation for the next pitch.

The Groove is an indentation of stone with a tiny seam in the back – the only weakness in an overhanging football field of smooth granite. Climbing it required that I build trust in tiny specialized equipment that fitted the two- to seven-millimetre-wide fissure. In some places, the fixed pitons in the crack were thinner than a penny, and the camming devices I placed were half the diameter of a tube of ChapStick. I made my way upward and tested each piece by aggressively bouncing on it in my aiders. It was better for a piece of hardware to release from the crack while I was close to the previous one, before I committed to top-stepping and reaching as high as I could to place the next bit of gear. I felt relaxed, well practised at physical courage. I rationalized that if I did fall, I could remain injury-free as long as I stayed tied into the rope – there was nothing to hit on the way down the blank, overhanging wall. My first Valley trip had taught me that falling is not a problem if the wall is clean and there are no rock features impeding downward motion. I theorized that if I really blew it somehow, I could be safe even after a 300-foot fall into thin air. With three bolts at the belay, I knew the main anchor would hold without fail.

I enjoyed the focus the pitch demanded. My attention stayed completely on assessing each tiny piece to hold my weight as I ascended, and I was happy to reach the next three-bolt anchor and fix myself firmly to the wall again. Once secured, my thoughts came back to our overall position in the rich sensory environment. Eric ascended the fixed line. I hauled the bags easily up the overhanging wall and got them to the anchor before Eric arrived.

The second crux pitch was the Triple Cracks, which look like three slightly overlapping pen strokes on a piece of paper, each line offset from the former by a couple of centimetres and ascending up the page. Eric deftly worked upward, making several difficult gear placements; the two of us like ants on a centurion's shield.

With time on my hands, I focused on the swallows that flew with speed and accuracy high up on the exposed face. I felt the intensity of the sun, softened by the convective wind that blew up from the valley far below.

I breathed in the ample fresh, clear air, seemingly as much below us as above.

The sound of Eric yelling "Off belay!" brought me back to the climbing. With him up the Triple Cracks, the hard parts of the route were complete. After one more pitch, we set up camp and organized our mass of equipment. So close to the top, we relaxed and enjoyed our last evening on the wall, eating and restoring our bodies for the final day ahead. I enjoyed the waning day, but again felt like I had blemished the climb with my previous outburst; with time on our hands that evening, I could have talked about it with Eric, but I let the opportunity pass.

The next day we passed Chicken Head Ledge and finished the climb.

At the top, I dumped out our haul bags to inventory what we had for dinner at our camp on the summit. A can of Campbell's Soup trundled out of the bag, escaped my grasp and bounced down the granite slab towards the void we had just spent four days climbing. At the last possible moment, it hit a tiny tree and landed securely in the well at its base, and I felt blessed with my luck. Eric gave me a simple belay using the rope and I went down to retrieve the soup. A weighty tin falling from such a great height could be fatal for a climber below. It would have been a terrible way to hurt someone, even though the chances of it actually connecting with a person were minimal. And with good fortune on my side, I even had my meal to eat that night on the summit.

As the sun dropped behind the horizon, we basked in the glow of the experience. For me it had been almost perfect.

I have taken wild physical risks in my life: rock climbs that resulted in big falls, alpine adventures with terribly loose rock, racing down icy slopes, climbing free-standing columns of frozen water, and of course skiing avalanche-prone slopes. When I count all of my near misses and tally them up, there are at least eleven times where I have come within a hair of dying in the mountains. But this only accounts for the occasions when my life was in danger and I was aware of it. I suspect the number would be higher if I were to include the times I have come close to death but have been completely oblivious to it. The eternal question that diligent mountaineers ponder is: for what purpose? The answer always consists of more than we can possibly understand, but it is important not to abandon the question because of an inability to come to any one definitive conclusion about it.

The first of near infinitely possible answers to that question for me is actually the opposite of courage: the mountains helped me to escape my family. By the age of 18, I searched for an escape from my life at home because it exerted a ton of pressure on me to be someone I was not. To me, adventure in the mountains was beautiful and exciting, and my high tolerance for physical risk may well have been a prolonged attempt at suicide.

My parents, and for me mostly my father, had a picture in their heads of who their children should be, and whenever that picture did not meet reality, they reacted negatively. Our teenage explorations of relationships, life's many questions and even music consistently met with judgment. Their criticisms made life almost unbearably stressful for their children, and unfortunately for all of us, some of their worst fears came true. There was a teen pregnancy, a mountain rescue of my brother Daryl, our gay brother Floyd ran away at 15 and was found unconscious in an alley in San Francisco, and Pat's drug use and self-directed violence. The harder our parents pushed, the more fervently we pushed back.

In 1982 Pat shot himself at point-blank range in his abdomen in our basement with a 12-gauge shotgun. He survived, but when the paramedics wheeled his blood-covered broken body through the house, my father said to him, "You can't even get this right – why didn't you put the gun in your mouth?"

That single comment blotted out all of the positive things he or my mother may ever have done; I labelled it all madness and wanted out. But rather than confront them I hightailed it to the mountains. The torment I felt about my family was the fuel I used to drive myself into new experiences, to test my capabilities and limits outside the reach of their authority and disapproval; if I died, I harshly rationalized, they would deserve losing me.

By default, I discovered something that I was willing to spend time mastering. When I eventually decided to make a career out of the outdoors, my dad's response to my path was utterly predictable: "When are you going to grow up and get a real job?" That only pushed me further, but once again, instead of confronting him face to face, I buried myself deeper in adventure.

From then on I missed family birthdays, was absent at Christmas for 14 years, and one of the quips I used when responding to invitations to attend family events was, "I'll come if it's raining." I imagined I was punishing them by being continually away on my cordilleran exploits.

Strangely, however, I retained a nagging desire to connect with them. I wanted them to notice what great things I was doing, to be curious about my efforts and the ways I was growing, especially my father. Each time nobody asked about my life on one of my few visits home, I would rush back to my mountain heights and medicate my suffering by taking increased risks, isolating myself even more and reinforcing the negative lesson that any attempt at forthright communication with people would at best result in failure, at worst in rejection and shunning, closing the circle of alienation even more.

Eventually I cultivated the belief that through exposure to physical risk I would develop courage. But my understanding of courage was like learning one word of a new language, and saying it over and again in a vain attempt to become fluent. Like my repeat figure-eleven runs at Paskapoo that had ended in failure, my constant misapplication of physical courage to social situations begged the need for a different approach. I made the choice to face my physical fear as I strode onto the slope of La Traviata, but the situation required the social courage I lacked to be the man I needed to be.

It all boiled down to this: I was at a point in my life where I was less afraid of the consequences of an avalanche than I was of confronting and being honest with other human beings. I had habituated myself to taking physical risks because I had become addicted to dodging social ones.

By writing this coming of age story, I found a yellow marble in the bed where I had lain in silence as a thirteen-year-old boy, looking at the picture of Scott Finlay's terrible crash, and put it in my other jar.

CHAPTER 7

LESSON THREE: CONNECTION

JUNE 1989

Our borrowed North Face VE-24 tent was perched on a flat spot on a glacial moraine at 13,000 feet in the Peruvian Andes, surrounded by snow and ice-plastered peaks. Jeff Nazarchuk and I had cooked and eaten our dinner of pasta and tuna as the equatorial sun dropped out of the sky, casting alpenglow on the peaks for our dessert. We spent our day organizing equipment and resting, since we had pushed hard the day before, carrying a load of food and gear to the toe of the glacier, at 16,000 feet. Our objective was to climb what the posters of the peak in the local towns touted as "the most beautiful mountain in the world" – Nevado Alpamayo. To test that claim was my sole purpose for climbing the peak.

Jeff and I had met working at a YMCA camp in the early 1980s on the east slope of the Canadian Rockies and, over time, struck up a powerful climbing partnership. Jeff, with his long sandy-brown hair and dark beard, looked exactly like a clichéd, Europeanized portrait of Jesus. I had hate in my heart for religion back then, but I was willing to believe in anything if it meant I could have a laugh. Our passion was climbing waterfall ice in the Canadian Rockies, and Jeff and I communicated well with a rope stretched between us and a challenge to face. I had experienced rapid success as an ice climber with Jeff. It had been like taking steroid injections: some of my parts grew quickly and others shrank, while climbing came first in my life, before any other relationships or commitments.

We had had a good rest day, but still feeling the effects of altitude we each popped a couple of Tylenols as we readied ourselves for bed, to remedy the slight headache caused by acute mountain sickness brought on by the thin air.

Men's voices approached; headlamps cast circular spots of light on the tan tent fabric from the outside. I fumbled with the zipper and parted the sturdy nylon door. Wearing lamps the diameter of an average pop can, two men poked their faces through the opening and introduced themselves as Hans and Christian from Austria. In a thick accent, Hans cut to the chase: "Von man his dead. Von man hass broken fooot. Can you help us?"

Jeff and I looked at each other and without words simultaneously nodded Yes. I was up for the adventure, and immediately saw how responding to a rescue up here would bring me social capital at home.

"Right now?" we asked.

"No," Hans said. "In da mornink."

Our splintered dialogue continued. We learned that three Swiss climbers had been near the top of the French Direct route on the southwest face of Alpamayo when tragedy struck. A cornice had collapsed, hitting two of them and sweeping them to the bottom of the face. Only one man survived.

Jeff and I had met these men the day before, decked out in flashy, bright-coloured European gear and heading for the French Direct route. We had exchanged simple greetings and basic interest at the base of the glacier. They had carried on to high camp at 18,000 feet, at the col between Alpamayo and Quitaraju, while we descended to our base, having cached our food and equipment.

Hans informed us that the situation was stable. The man with the broken leg had made it back to a tent at high camp but needed our help to get down the next day. The four of us planned to meet at 7 a.m., and Hans and Christian left Jeff and me to prepare our paraphernalia and psyches for the early start. Our greatest concern was that we would have to climb to 18,000 feet to help the injured man, when neither of us had been that high ever before. I was excited, drawn to the drama of the situation; my ego revelled in what I believed was "the real game."

We had come to Peru on Jeff's initiative; I lacked the curiosity to conceive my own projects in those days. Photocopied *Canadian Alpine Journal* articles about Nevado Alpamayo and Nevado Cayesh arrived in the mail from him while I was working in Tahoe at a cross-country ski camp with Nancy. A Post-it note stuck to the pages simply said: "Want to climb these?" By mid-June we boarded the rickety early-model Aeroperú 727 in Los Angeles.

I spent the entire flight to Lima with a sore ass from a gamma globulin shot I received in each butt cheek the day before. Following the first injection the immunization nurse asked, "How long are you going?" When I said, "Six weeks," she replied, "Roll over." After finishing her work with me, she asked me out to dinner; the encounter became something I boasted about.

We were two 24-year-olds from "Cowtown," Alberta, with no clue about the outside world, having never visited other cultures. At the Lima airport, taxi drivers crowded around us, projecting their voices in desperation to get a fare. We were warned that they wanted to take us to "their" hotel, one that offered them a cut for bringing new guests. The dark ride through the lamp-less streets of Lima mirrored my underlit view of Peruvians. I sat in the back of the cab cultivating negativity, assuming the driver would take advantage of us somehow, just because he was "foreign" to me.

Sleep was fitful in our dirty white concrete-walled room with its single bare light bulb; the gunshots that rang out in the middle of the night did little to ease our insomnia. We knew a bit about the Maoist insurgent group the Sendero Luminoso (the Shining Path), including the fact that they were highly active in 1989, randomly blowing up capitalist establishments. As our awareness of their presence grew, my sole concern was that they not inhibit our plans to climb. We had heard that they hid out in some of the valleys of the Cordillera.

In the morning we roamed the streets of Lima, our senses experiencing the sulphurous smell of rancid meat cooking; the sight of green, red and blue liquids in bottles at the hot drink vendor; hearing the fast-spoken Spanish of the Peruvian black-market money-changers, calculators in hand; and the overt distress of some of the people. All of it fuelled my mistrust. Lima exposed a raw side of life with few buffers, which Jeff and I observed rather than participated in. There was one thread that we did exploit: people in the street called Jeff "Jesús," pronounced "Hey-Seus" under their breath as if word was spreading of the Second Coming. We loved the power this gave us in our seemingly powerless situation.

We took an afternoon nap to rest from the morning of over-stimulation, and boarded a night bus for the mountain town of Huaraz, located on the Pacific side of the Andean range called the Cordillera Blanca (White Mountains). It was a 12-hour ride up the dry, rain-shadowed western slope of the Andes, beginning at 6:00 p.m. The hard, right-angled seats of the Chevrolet school bus, while practical for delivering children to school, were penitential for an overnight ride. The driver made numerous nocturnal stops at small dustbowl villages, where the local people joined the journey: women costumed in black skirts and dark felt hats, often carrying a chicken under an arm, which we laughed about; men in slacks, dress shirts and black leather shoes carrying nothing; and small boys selling mandarin oranges.

The kids were brazen little creatures and I noticed during my stay that I never saw a Peruvian kid cry. Even the hardest blow from an older brother produced only laughter. Today I still marvel at their resiliency. One boy held a plastic bag of oranges up to our faces as we dozed, slumped in our miserable seats, and barked in his high, prepubescent voice, "Gringo! Mandarina!" I strived to nurture compassion for him, because at age five he was up in the middle of the night, doing his damnedest to earn some money. We bought the oranges, but my darker side just wanted the little urchin to go away. I wondered about people who travel to other countries and really connect with the locals. I had a wall around me ... afraid of making a connection because it might lead to the responsibility a relationship requires. I suspected they sensed my fear.

The nocturnal endurance test deposited us in Huaraz, a bustling mountain town at the toe of the Andes. Trundling off the bus in the bright morning sun, we found a man with a wooden-chassis bike cart to transport our bags. "Mucho peso," he said as he hefted each duffle or pack onto his mini flatbed, its light frame straining under the load. We wanted to find Edward's Inn, owned by a mountain guide named Eduardo Figueroa, the place where climbers gathered. The man with the bags crushing his cart nodded affirmation of our destination, saying, "Si, si," and off we went. The trek took us on a circuitous route through the side streets of Huaraz, rich with bright-coloured Andean weavings, seas of dark hair and the alternating smells of urine and unrefrigerated meat.

Inside the walls of the Edward's Inn courtyard we found shelter from the sensory overload of the streets and Edward's whole family at our service. The brick fortifications were there to protect against the Sendero Luminoso, because Edward's was a capitalist establishment. The ramparts with their glass shards cemented on top mirrored my own walls: a place where I felt safe, but alone and isolated from the world.

Jeff and I settled in and began our acclimatization, hiking each day into the surrounding hills and giving our bodies a chance to adjust to the thin Andean air. The body, at least, adapts wonderfully to environmental stress – with less oxygen in the air, it produces more red blood cells to carry more of it to meet demand. En route back to Edward's in the afternoons we purchased food and bits of gear and made a fruitless search for plastic bags.

After a few days, more accustomed to the thin air, we hired a collectivo to take us to our trailhead for the Santa Cruz valley. In Cashapampa, at the foot of the valley, after the requisite ceremonial negotiations, we hired Pedro, an arriero, or donkey driver, to help us transport our food and equipment on our three-week journey to attempt Alpamayo. The Santa Cruz landscape was a breath of freedom after the stressful days navigating the towns and dealing with transport and logistics. A bewitching panorama of peaks formed the horizon as we hiked up the gentle U-shaped valley. The basin, a place nearly devoid of trees, provided a clear vista of the striking Taulliraju at its head. Our eyes were pulled to a southwest buttress as we got progressively closer to it, coveting the idea of climbing it.

The first night, we camped at Laguna Jatuncocha, where Jeff and I shared our tent with Pedro, a desperately poor man. I was reticent to sleep next to him, afraid of his humanity, poverty and smell, as if being too close to him would harm me in some way.

After two days of walking, Pedro deposited our food and gear where Quebrada Arhuaycocha poured into the main Santa Cruz drainage. Moments after being paid Pedro made tracks for home, the exchange for him and us being strictly business. As he walked away he never looked back.

Pedro's return home left us in a daunting void: just Jeff, myself and our gear, surrounded by a powerful and unknown range. We filled the emptiness with the work of organizing ourselves, spreading our gear out over the well-pastured grass to verify everything. While going through the climbing hardware, Jeff discovered a partial hairline crack in my right crampon behind the front points. He asked, "Why didn't you check these at home?" My shrug was not the answer he sought, yet inside I was reeling with fear knowing that Jeff could see the real me: the person who is not as diligent as he could be.

I pretended it was not a big deal, but inside I beat up on myself, thinking only that my damaged crampon could compromise the success of the trip. I barely considered that my oversight had left our safety now undermined. The prospect of Jeff's judgment was much more terrifying than dealing with the situation honestly. For the most part Jeff was a vehicle for me to get where I wanted to go, and I did not want to lose that resource. My social interactions with him were strictly conversations about conquests of climbs or women. I did not know how to go deeper, to a more meaningful place.

When we received the visit from the Austrians, camped on the moraine of Alpamayo, our daily rhythm had consisted of acclimatizing to the thin air by ferrying our gear from the valley to the mountain. Now, after their visit, we slept poorly in anticipation of the upcoming rescue. Morning came, and four men – Hans, Christian, Hans and Olivier – arrived at our camp from the valley below. Olivier Roduit was the man who had come down from the mountain to summon our assistance via the Austrians; now the six of us were the rescue team for Pierrot.

After greetings and introductions we strode up the

moraine with light packs, our ski poles clicking on the stones to provide stability. Balancing up the knife-edge moraine, I asked Olivier what had happened. In a measured Swiss accent, he replied, "The three off us were on the French Direct route that goes straight up the southwest face to the summit of Alpamayo. I was anchored, ten metres from the top. It was a good anchor; I slung a large ice pillar. I was belaying Pierrot and Christophe up the ice when the summit cornice released above me to the right. The avalanche of snow missed me and funnelled down, right into Pierrot and Christophe. The force from the snow on the two men broke the climbing ropes where they redirected over a carabiner at the belay. Both Pierrot and Christophe fell the entire 350 metres down the face, with most of the rope trailing behind them. I remained at the top, with only a few metres of rope, and I could see the two of them lying on the snow at the bottom of the route. I had no choice but to downclimb the face without a rope, to get to them. The difficult part was the bergschrund; I had to jump over it and hope to land safely on the other side. When I arrived at the bottom, it was clear that Christophe was dead. Pierrot, unbelievably, only had a broken lower leg. I assisted him in making the 400 metres to the tent at high camp. Then I helped him to be as comfortable as possible and descended alone, down the glacier and moraine, to the valley bottom. There I was able to alert the Austrians, who came to you last night."

I steered away from condolences, afraid that saying

something might bring on a cascade of emotion. Instead I kept the exchange technical and shared my fascination with the fact that the ropes had broken over a carabiner.

A long journey up the moraine and glacier brought us to high camp, just over the Alpamayo–Quitaraju col, where Pierrot lay waiting in the tiny tent. I was light-headed from lack of oxygen so I needed to stay on task and descend as soon as possible. I knew I had to be honest with myself about what less oxygen at that altitude was doing to my body and respond appropriately, saying to Jeff, "I have not got much time up here so I'll start making anchors for the descent." I turned inward and let the others take action on the rescue.

The Austrians, who were able to communicate with Pierrot, managed his needs, getting him food and water. We collectively decided to commit Christophe's body to a crevasse in the glacier as a final resting place, brashly thinking that since he was from a mountaineering family, his next of kin would accept such a "burial." Given our perceived lack of resources, we decided it too dangerous to haul his remains down and that instead, getting Pierrot off the mountain was our primary concern. The Austrians bundled him and his broken leg into a climbing harness, a sleeping bag and a nylon tarp, readying him for lowering down the steep snow slope below the col to the east.

While a team of three went to push Christophe's corpse into the crevasse, I busied myself building a T-slot anchor. With the adze of my ice axe I cut a 70 cm deep trough in the snow, perpendicular to our line of descent. Then at the midpoint I cut another ascending trough that pointed toward the line of descent. With a clove hitch I secured a sling to a ski pole section, placed the assembly into the bar of the T and backfilled the entire trench with snow, stomping it hard, leaving a sling loop on the surface. I was unsure about the strength of the pole, so backfilling helped boost my confidence. Once the first one was complete I descended, building an anchor every fifty metres.

The team above lowered Pierrot down the steep, icy slope just below the col, guided by two rescuers, following my lead. I watched the group of men above use my anchors, shocked at the number of people loading them. There were many stress-filled minutes as I looked on in amazement that it was all holding. After several pitches of descent, Pierrot was at the bottom of the steepest part of the route down. It was relatively easy for the makeshift stretcher to slide down the remaining glacier. When Pierrot showed some discomfort, we made adjustments to make him as comfortable as possible until we arrived at the glacier's toe.

At the end of the glacial ice, the rescue shifted gears; Pierrot did not want us to carry him over the rocks, fearing it would expose his rescuers to undue hazard. He was able to take his weight with one leg and, with assistance, slowly make his way down. Given their glacial pace and the waning daylight, Olivier and Pierrot chose to bivouac not far from the toe of the glacier and finish the descent in the morning, rather than rush and make a mistake. I was eager to get down, enticed by the lush green valley below that I knew contained food, water and rest.

At camp, we dispatched an arriero to Cashapampa to bring in horses for Pierrot and Olivier to ride out on from their base camp. Everyone rested and ate a meal in the Austrians' large kitchen tent. Our conversation was limited while we ate, since neither Jeff nor I spoke Austrian-German, failing to acknowledge that on the mountain, with our technical systems and climbing skills, we all spoke the same language.

As night fell, Jeff and I hiked back to our own base camp and collapsed in our sleeping bags, exhausted from the efforts of the day but feeling more at home in this range, like we had just experienced the heart of the place.

Jeff and I strolled down the moraine from our camp and into the Austrians' wall tent after a night's rest, to discover that Olivier and Pierrot had safely arrived at base. Representatives from Peru, Canada, Switzerland and Austria sat around a large table and savoured cheese, salty salami and boiled baby potatoes slathered with butter – the meal a welcome change from our dried provisions and Knorr soup. The mood was happy for most of us, but I could see the weight of the event on the faces of Pierrot and Olivier as they orbited the outside of the group. Jeff and I gravitated to the camaraderie of the inner circle instead of comforting them – for me that was far beyond what was possible at the time.

Later that afternoon, several men arrived from the Casa de Guias (Mountain Guides' House "office"), led by Eduardo Figueroa. From Eduardo, we learned that Christophe's body was to be collected; his family wanted his resting place to be in Switzerland. Peruvian mountain guides would do the work of going up and retrieving his body from the crevasse over the coming days. Jeff and I watched with interest as people haggled over Christophe's gear – one man even said, "These boots go really well with the skis," trying to secure the whole set of equipment for himself.

With some assistance, Pierrot mounted a horse shortly after breakfast, and soon he and Olivier were on their way to civilization and medical care.

We waved goodbye, and as they departed in their bright Gore-Tex all I could muster from my thoughts was how silly they looked next to the more appropriately attired gaucho.

Their departure spawned an exodus of nearly all the others. Once again Jeff and I were alone, tasked with remustering momentum for our journey up Alpamayo. Given the circumstances, we considered the idea of going rock climbing in Squamish instead, but decided to continue with our expedition. The thought of quitting was not an option for me – I was a climber, not yet a person who climbed. I did not want to let the event get in the way of achieving what I had come to do.

Our itinerary evolved into acclimatizing while ascending a more straightforward route on Quitaraju before attempting the Ferrari Route on Alpamayo. The Ferrari Route was to the left of the line the Swiss had taken, and we chose it out of fear of climbing where the Swiss had been simply by reason of association, not logic.

Our momentum gathered while we packed equipment and food. My crampon had worked during the rescue and its hairline crack showed no sign of worsening, but it was still a source of stress. I had lacked the simple human courage to ask Pierrot and Olivier for Christophe's crampons (which I'm sure they would gladly have given me), even though it would have made the climb safer for both Jeff and me.

Our packs were loaded and ready for schlepping, when a day party of Peruvian mountain guides passed us on their way to retrieve Christophe's body from the crevasse. They marched by, looking fit and strong, while Jeff and I focused our energy on simply making it to high camp. We hiked for several hours, retracing our steps up the moraine and the glacier, the track well compacted from our descent with Pierrot days before. Though heavily laden, we felt strong and capable, knowing we had already been this high.

On the snowy bench just below the steep climb to the col, the Peruvian guides hauled Christophe's lifeless body past us. A stiff arm stuck out of its green nylon tarp wrapping, his wrist and gold watch visible. We stopped and shared a wordless examination of each other and then turned our attention back to the corpse. The destructive power of the Andes lay there in the snow before us. Standing there on the glacier, I pushed the thought of death far away from my realm of possibility. Sadly, I felt nothing for the man, only the fear that if I felt anything for him at all, I might lose my motivation and have to go home. I watched the scene, but all I saw was a perfectly good pair of crampons sliding by me and on down to the valley.

Steady effort brought us to the col at 18,000 feet. The panorama of Alpamayo, Quitaraju and the Cordillera Blanca was a breathtaking reward in the late-afternoon light. Perched there on the cold, hard-packed snow, we felt the silent power of the place.

With a burst of energy we set up the tent, lit the stove to make water from snow and embraced the long process of taking care of ourselves: drying our gear, resting, eating and hydrating our bodies. Our normal rapid movements did not work so well in the thin air. I suffered from chronic dysentery but carried on as if not bothered by anything. We peered up the steep, fluted, intimidating southwest face of Alpamayo. I muffled the knowledge of how a mountain can act with cold, callous indifference with humour and worked hard to turn anything into a laugh. We crawled into our tent when the shadows grew long and cold. Finally I wormed my way into my massive sleeping bag and lay down to rest.

The entire next day we relaxed in the warm sunshine,

feeling our bodies grow strong with rest and rehydration. The next tick, Quitaraju, was an easy ascent that put us on a classic alpine face and then a ridge, an event that was not without incident. On the descent, I tripped on the knife-edged summit ridge, hooking the heel point of my crampon on the wrist-loop of a mountaineering axe I had carelessly left dangling from my backpack. Jeff and I were short-roping; he saw the event unfold and arrested my stumble before it even registered for me. It was without question a life-saving manoeuvre on his part, given our position.

As we continued our climb, a group of three pitched their tent next to ours at the col: Canadians Paul Berntsen and Lisa Richardson, and their friend Kate from California. Fast friends, we determined that Paul and Lisa would climb behind us on Alpamayo. Kate's aim was to enjoy high camp.

We laughed, played Crazy Eights and hung around inside all the next day drinking tea while the afternoon produced a series of thunder and graupel (winter hail) storms. Downtime brought strength and further adjustment of our bodies to the thin air.

In the pre-dawn blackness, I lit the stove in the vestibule of the tent and made breakfast. While choking down my oatmeal, I felt the typical competing emotions of dread and excitement that define these moments. Thoughts of the Swiss climbers tumbling down the face replayed in my mind, but at no point did I think of the loss or grief their families were feeling, or the concern of my own family back home. Concern for others was just not there – my greatest fear was simply of dying, followed closely by going home without summiting. After stoking our bodies with food and water, we put our harnesses and helmets on in the tent to keep our fingers warm. We were ready for the southwest face of Alpamayo.

Both teams made our way across the upper bench below the looming southwest face, our headlamps gleaming on the squeaky solid track; Paul and Lisa were not far behind us. The crisp morning air bit at toes, fingers and nostrils. The icy, gargoyled face loomed above, protected by the moat-like bergschrund, a crevasse that marks the border between the unmoving alpine ice of the peak and the glacier below it, which flows down-valley by the sheer weight of its snow and ice accumulation. As dawn crept up we surmounted the difficult upper wall of the 'schrund and climbed up the 60-degree snow and ice face. The new day's light conceived uncountable shades of blue that melded the snow and the sky together. We gauged our gathering height against Quitaraju as the day progressed, slowly matching its stature with each move up the icy face.

Our position on the wall was indefensible, cornices loomed above and I felt my senses heighten. Our early start was in part to get ahead of the afternoon thunder squalls we'd experienced on previous days. Climbers are at risk in the high alpine – like a golfer climbing atop a tree in a lightning storm. We were on a slope that was too steep to avalanche: snow slides down the face immediately after it falls out of the sky, never accumulating any significant mass, save for in cornices on the ridge.

Ten centimetres of firm supportive snow on top of the ice made for good, comfortable footing that kept me off my weak front crampon point. We swung leads: the first person climbed a pitch, placing one screw midway and anchoring with two ice screws at fifty metres to bring up the second climber.

Fluted snow 70 degrees steep, together with the gathering clouds, guarded the summit. Jeff led, making no comment about the difficulty. From the belay I could easily see his struggle; he had a near-impossible time finding solid ice for tool placements and ice screw protection, but somehow made his way, move by move, up the pitch. In time, he stepped up to the sun on the summit ridge. His elation registered in my ears and communicated that he was on top. I followed his lead and felt the difficulty of the pitch. My feet skittered trying to find solid ice for my crampons to bite into, and I struggled with my ice tools, swinging them repeatedly to find purchase in the cohesion-less recrystallized snow. My lungs screamed, unsatiated in the thin air, but the difficulty ended when I arrived at the ridge with a better understanding of the mountain.

Jeff and I stood on the summit ridge, as narrow as a steeply pitched house roof, at 19,500 feet. From our standpoint the mountain plunged away on all sides and we were elated to see, through the mist to the east, the surrounding peaks and jungle forest below.

In minutes, Paul and Lisa joined us on the ridge, giving us a completely unwarranted sense of safety by having them nearby. The company and conversation took my mind off the danger of our position. With the ridge that led to the top clearly inundated with crashing waves of snow too hazardous to negotiate, we called our location the summit. I snapped a picture of Jeff in his white Edelrid helmet with the sticker on it saying "Damn, I'm good!" and we began our descent.

Looking down our line of ascent brought my mind back to the fall of the Swiss climbers and caused my stomach to flip. I built a solid T-slot at the top and committed myself to gravity in our team of four for the descent. On the icy face we hammered in electrical conduit loosely backed up with a screw for rappel anchors, for the first people down. I tried to avoid being the last person, who had to rappel without the backup. An hour later, we arrived back on the flat bench as the sun illuminated the southwest face, its equatorial intensity compromising the strength of the snow.

To minimize our exposure to a cornice collapse, Jeff and I transitioned the rope quickly from descent to glacier-travel mode. Moving out from below the face, and with snow balling up in our cookie-cutter crampons, we embarked on a molasses-like trudge up the little hill to our sun-filled camp. We were elated to be back, having climbed the face without incident.

After a hard night of headaches, our plan was to descend to base camp for a rest. Not wanting to have to down climb with a big pack, I suggested to Jeff that he lower me with the packs down the steepest part of the headwall below the col to the east, which would allow him to descend easily without a pack. He agreed, we rigged the ropes and I was on my way. Halfway down, I upended in deep soft snow, and Jeff kept paying out rope. With slack building up in the system, the weight of the two packs transferred to me. I feared falling with them, anger boiling in me as the rope continued to pile up between the slope and me. I yelled, "Jeff, stop!" There was no response. Assuming he was being careless, I yelled again. "JEFFFFF – FUUUUCKING ... STOOOOP!!!" The rope kept looping down onto me like a thin stream of fudge on top of a sundae.

Realizing that my well-being was now entirely up to me, I found my balance on the steep slope, then wrestled one pack off the line and unclipped it from the system. It trundled freely down the snowy slope, gaining impressive speed and momentum before stopping breathtakingly close to a crevasse. I shouldered Jeff's pack and began my descent down the steep but easy slope, angrily kicking my feet into snow that bottomed out in ice.

When Jeff caught up, I accosted him: "What the hell were you doing? That was horrendous! The packs were yanking me down the face! Couldn't you feel that my weight was off the rope when I got into the deeper snow?"

"I didn't feel you at all. There was so much friction over the snow edge. I couldn't hear anything either because of the distance and the wind up at the col, so I just paid rope out."

"That was fuckin' stupid. Just stupid," I said, seeing it all as only his mistake.

"Sorry, man," said Jeff, looking confused and more than a little hurt.

I had projected onto Jeff my own failure to trust myself on the down climb. He was a whipping post there for my use when I needed to vent, but nothing more.

Amends made, we descended to the valley in need of rest and recuperation. We spent a couple of days relaxing, eating and making repairs to our bodies and kit.

Jeff and Paul then made an ascent of Artesonraju, a beautiful peak across the valley that we all decided looks exactly like the peak used by Paramount Pictures in their logo. I started out with them but turned back, ill from the effects of dysentery. Lisa and Kate opted to hang out in camp and rest. A day after their return we hiked out. On the walk back to Cashapampa I had opportunity to reflect on my experience. There was nothing left to do but walk; I could have thought about my failure to connect with myself and others on that trip, but the lesson I brought home was the opposite of what I most craved.

In Cashapampa, Paul, Lisa, Kate, Jeff and I binged by eating a whole chicken each, drinking copious Cristal beer and smoking heavy-duty cigarettes. Groggy, we made it back to Huaraz to eat ice cream at Crêperie Patrick by midday.

I always told this story differently before reflecting on what the Andes showed me about myself. If I said anything, it used to be something like "I climbed Alpamayo; we responded to a rescue while we were there." I never talked about my systematic self-isolation from everyone who was there with me.

I wove a different tale about La Traviata in the early days after that tragedy too. I had allowed a terrifying ocean to roil between Ruedi and me in the weeks, days and moments before the catastrophe, which led in part to its cause. I was afraid to share what I was sure would be perceived as my weaknesses, and in so doing I let them develop into something much bigger than they ever should have been.

Standing just above Tumbledown Lake, as I looked across our group of people to Ruedi, my heart screamed at me to close the rift. Today I can only guess where my efforts would have led, perhaps to being "shut down" by him for my efforts to communicate that I believed we were heading for disaster. But that does not matter, I now know; at least I would have tried.

I found a purple marble while writing about my 1989 trip to Peru with Jeff. I discovered it during my heartless exchange with him after the lowering incident. It will, now saved in my other jar, work to shape how I act and interact with people in my remaining days. It reminds me that the key ingredient to human connection is allowing oneself to be vulnerable.[9] I do not expect it will make me perfect, but hopefully at least more aware. All of the efforts I made struggling up those snowy and icy sides of Alpamayo are now redolent with meaning.

CHAPTER 8

LESSON FOUR: SELF-DISCOVERY

On a winter night in 1987, I was lying in bed at my parents' home in southwest Calgary, ruminating on deep feelings of inadequacy, trying to envision what it would feel like to do something significant in my life. Like so many other times before, I fantasized about the respect that others would afford me if I could do something spectacular, so I hatched a plan to solo an ice climb called Polar Circus. At 1:00 a.m., I jumped out of bed and packed my gear to escape my valley bottom.

The mountain valleys of the Canadian Rockies are U-shaped, with flat floors and steep sides: a geomorphology shaped by the flowing, many-kilometres-thick glaciers of the ice age over ten thousand years ago. The peaks consist primarily of sedimentary rock, prone to hanging water tables and shale basins that feed seepages producing waterfalls that freeze in winter. Since the age of seven, I have been enamoured of the idea and the act of climbing frozen waterfalls. Some ice routes are close to the valley bottoms, embraced by magical conifer forest with moss and lichen, while others are high in the desolate limestone cliffs of the alpine. There are a plethora of routes in Canada that I now call a dojo for waterfall ice climbing.

Polar Circus is a classic representative among the hundreds. The route is located on Cirrus Mountain along the Icefields Parkway, the highway that links Lake Louise and Jasper, Alberta. Polar Circus is inviting yet unnerving at the same time. What makes it welcoming to climbers is that it consists of a series of tiers with ledges in between. Each section has its own character as the route turns and twists up the mountain, affording its climbers constantly changing perspectives on their way up. Ascending a single pitch is like walking through some grand doorway in a castle that takes one into a powerful new room to explore – in this case, chambers of snow and ice.

What makes it equally unnerving is that the upper pitches get progressively more difficult to climb, and there are eight avalanche start zones in the often snow-laden basins above that funnel down the drainage.

Once finished packing my equipment, I drove over to Jim Preston's apartment on the University of Calgary campus. It was 2:00 a.m. when I knocked on his door. Despite the hour, he answered in his usual cheerful way, "Hello, Ken, how can I help you?"

"I'm off to solo Polar Circus and I need a second rope to get down. Can I borrow your 9 mm?"

"Of course," Jim said, and in his habitually generous way added, "Is there anything else you need? Screws or pins?" I said no and apologized for waking him in the middle of the night.

"No worries, mate. Are you sure there is nothing more you need?"

"No, I have everything now," I replied, and thanked him. Failing to see an example of the respect I myself sought standing right there before me, I turned my back on him without another thought and headed out the door, rope in hand.

I drove my '73 orange Olds Omega, "The Pumpkin," up the massive glacial valley of the Bow River, past other classic waterfalls like Professors and the newly climbed Terminator on Mount Rundle, right above the townsite of Banff. I had climbed Professors many times, enjoying the journey up pitches wrapped by forest on either side, but Terminator was a new and desperately difficult route, high in the rocky alpine, that was far beyond my ability. I carried on past Lake Louise and up the Icefields Parkway to the picnic shelter, just southeast of the Weeping Wall pullout, at Polar Circus. The mountain world outside the car felt harsh, desolate, powerful, inviting and beautiful all at once.

With The Pumpkin left running to keep me warm, I dressed and put on my boots: the ritual of getting ready to climb. I have always enjoyed the "psych" of getting into my gear, likening it to becoming battle-ready. Filled with fear, I could only think about how climbing this route solo could change my life. With boots on, equipment ready and headlamp illuminating my way, I left the car in the pre-dawn and hiked up the lightly trodden snow path with the previous day's crampon marks on it to the base of the climb.

There I felt a different kind of cold from the penetrating humidity of the moist ice at the foot of the first blue curtain. I flaked out the ropes to trail behind me, put my harness, helmet and crampons on, threaded my hands through the ice-tool leashes and then began climbing, alone in my own little world, the tiniest of specks in the massive terrain that lay above me.

I found my rhythm on the first pitches. The climbing was well within my ability, but I was remembering all the while that on Polar Circus it gets more difficult as one gets higher. On the Ribbon Pitch, still 130 metres from the top, I hit my wall: an aerated section of ice where I could not get the solid tool placements I desired to feel secure enough to move upward. I repeated my attempts to move off the ledge numerous times, only to find wobbly hooks for the picks of my Stubai tools. A voice inside me said, "No, the risk is too much, turn back."

Frustrated and furious, back on the ledge on the right side of the climb, I clipped into the anchor in the rock and all of the memories of the failures in my life flooded into me: troubles with school, lost loves and feeling I never fit in anywhere. The pain of these events overwhelmed me as I squatted in torment, unable to even accept, much less value, "the voice" that was keeping me from harming myself.

In despair, I rappelled down the route, hiked back to the car and stripped off my gear, disgusted with myself for having returned to my valley bottom after my "failed" attempt at the ascent. The three-hour drive back to the University of Calgary took me past all of the beautiful places I still dreamed of climbing, and I gave Jim his rope back without saying a word. But I did report my attempt at the route to others in the Outdoor Centre on campus, and watched myself lie about the height I achieved, claiming I got to the crux before I turned around.

I could have reported that I had abandoned the climb when I realized it was no longer safe for me to carry on, but that was not enough. It was not enough because all I could think about was that I had "failed." I did not know how to stand in my own truth about things and have that be sufficient, not only when conditions forced me to turn around, but also when things went perfectly and I was able to complete a challenge.

WINTER 1996–97

Ten years later, after having disappeared for a decade, The Terminator formed once more, along with two other immediately adjacent frozen waterfalls, The Replicant and Sea of Vapours. With the same ongoing hope of gaining the attention of others from my accomplishments, I journeyed to the north side of Mount Rundle, high above Banff townsite in the valley.

During my second year of ice climbing, in 1986, these routes had been far beyond my ability; in those days, the ice hanging off Mount Rundle was at the edge of what was possible to scale even for the best climbers in the world. There was a buzz in the climbing community the year The Terminator first formed; we used to call it The Drip. Some locals had their eyes on it, but in 1985 Craig Reason and Jay Smith came up from the States and climbed it, and in so doing they changed its name from The Drip to The Terminator.

In the intervening decade, The Terminator had failed to form completely, but I climbed a lot of ice, not exclusively in preparation for The Terminator in the front of my mind, but certainly in the back of it. Through those years, the legend about the route grew. I remember driving with Joe Josephson in his now infamous silver Subaru to a climb in Field, British Columbia, about eight years after the first ascent of The Terminator. As we passed Mount Rundle, driving below it on Highway 1, the conversation turned to the notion of an ascent. Between spitting his sunflower seeds into his dirty coffee cup, eyeglasses sitting slightly askew on his face, Joe said, "Yeah, I know what that climb is all about (spit, spit) – three pitches that will fry my arms."

In early winter of 1996–97, a report from Paul Valiulis

and Joe McKay, who had wandered up there to check conditions, said that they had gone right up to the base of The Terminator, and that it was big, fat and climbable again ... though very wet. Keith Haberl, Richard Jagger (Jagg) and I decided to assume the challenge.

Heeding Paul and Joe's observation, we prepared ourselves for getting wet. We brought a light 7 mm tag line for quickly hauling up a daypack with extra layers, along with two ropes, ice screws for protection, and all the other technical equipment. Our attention to detail was of the highest order: we agonized over the smallest item. I spent Thursday night before the climb in Canmore, away from my home in Calgary, to get an early start and begin the climb on Friday instead of on the weekend, having adjusted my work schedule at Mount Royal College.

On the dark approach, our headlamps illuminating the sparkling snow, the green conifers and the path ahead, I repeated Joe's words in my mind, personalizing them: "Three pitches that will fry my arms." In keen anticipation, I quickened my pace.

Nearing the wall of the mountain's Palliser limestone, I felt its imposing nature. That wall was like the towers of a basilica, designed to induce reverence in those who approached or even passed by, its power amplified by the terrain below, which fell away, untreed, for a thousand feet down to the forest, then on to the Bow River in the valley. My inner voice felt strong and true in this place of intimidation; "Keep going," it said.

When we reached a protected alcove at the base of the climb, there was quiet among us for the first few minutes as we each turned inward to find our focus. Then Jagg cracked a joke that released the emotions welled up inside us all. In fifteen minutes we tightened our boots and put on harnesses, helmets and crampons. I double-checked my ice tools to see that the picks were tight and my leashes were perfect. Collectively we decided to climb the approach pitch without a rope for protection. The decision was a good one because it facilitated the speed of our ascent and sharpened our attention for the terrain ahead.

As we climbed side by side, I saw Jagg look up at the free-standing pillar of The Terminator above; foreboding registered on his face.

"Try not to look at it from here," I suggested gently. "These things look terrifying from directly below." Keith, on the other side of me, battled the brittle ice and said, "Good thing this is just the easy bit. Because my arms are already pumped." Both of them articulated the nervousness I felt, but there was no pull from inside me to turn around. My heart was there, in the midst of some of the biggest ice climbing terrain in the world, and no place else.

The brittle, undulating ice yielded to a slope at its top and then to the base of Terminator Wall. We stood in a three-point stance to look up at the face without losing our balance; the windless air registered –10° C on my face. The route up was beautiful – a long column of vertical and overhanging ice in innumerable shades of teal and blue, stretching 150 metres above where we stood. There were roof features with icicles hanging from them, and cauliflower pedestals dotted the column: a beauty rare for humans to behold.

My eyes searched for the line of least resistance; intimidation morphed into excitement as I recognized the vulnerabilities of the column and imagined climbing it with their assistance. My eager determination did not wane even though the route was, as reported, streaming with water. Our options were to climb it wet or go home and run the risk of waiting another ten years for the column to re-form. We chose wet. The possibility that the opportunity for the climb might last the whole season, and that the column might be dry later, never entered the conversation. We were here *now*.

Socially, I elbowed my way into leading the first pitch by simply volunteering. Cold seeped into my body as I readied my equipment, meticulously organizing ice screws and slings on my harness. With a figure-eight knot I tied into two ropes, while Keith and Jagg connected into the opposite ends of each. I then clipped a thin-diameter line to the back of my harness – the creative link to dry layers once we arrived sodden at the top of our pitch.

After a spiralling wrap behind the free-standing pillar, with the ropes running below me, I drilled a screw into solid ice and clipped the ropes to it for protection. Diligent in placing my tools and positioning my feet, I traversed out to the front of the column and committed to the ice-cold shower. Haste was my ally to minimize my exposure to the ice water. I heard the spatter of its drops on my helmet. When I looked up for tool placements, water falling at high speed collided with my corneas, hurting my eyeballs and blurring my vision. The steep climb put inordinate strain on my arms. Ice water found its way in at my wrists overhead and trickled to my elbows, armpits and then ribs and hips. The situation was outwardly desperate, but inside I felt calm and self-assured. I climbed quickly, embracing upward progression against physical factors that tried to convince me to give up. I had no idea how I would sustain this physical effort for the length of the pitch. I moved up into the unknown guided only by a voice inside that shouted: "You can do this!"

A few more taxing moves up I discovered that the ice pillar contained an alcove like a vertical dugout canoe. I stepped inside, grateful to balance on my feet as the water streamed harmlessly behind me. Soaked, I kept moving to stay warm and pliable.

Climbing up the tube itself was fun and easier than I could have hoped. I stemmed and bridged like Santa in a chimney, my spiked feet pressing against opposite ice walls to ease the load on my arms. There were plenty of opportunities to protect my ascent by placing screws in the ice and clipping my rope to them. Having been worried about "frying my arms" for years, I felt this opportunity was a steal and yelled down, "This is easy!" Keith and Jagg, staring up at the daunting pillar, unaware of its rich secrets, burst out laughing.

At the top of the hollow cylinder, an overhang blocked the way to the steep ice above. After placing another screw, I bridged my feet up, reached around right, and swung to place a solid tool up at two o'clock. I shifted my feet to the right and in line below the new tool to form a stable tripod from which to swing the next tool. The progress brought me back into the icy shower; after advancing one more move, I reduced my exposure to the heavy spray by shifting further right, navigating to find what I needed. One step too far to the right I found brittle ice; my tool released a dinner-plate-size chunk of it, which bounced off my right foot, then drifted down silently until it contacted the ledge below. *BOOOF!* A few centimetres left, I found the sweet spot of the climb, where most of my ice tool placements were as effortless as stabbing a block of aged cheddar cheese. Water cascaded down further to my left, trickling and spattering down the undulating frozen surface.

A couple of body lengths of vertical, featureless ice brought me to a cave that I entered on the right, stepping up onto its ledge as if getting out of a swimming pool. With urgency, I anchored myself to two screws and hauled up the green daypack that contained dry clothing. After stripping to the skin, I re-layered and was instantly warm and cozy. Then I threaded the rope through the belay device and anchored it to the two screws to protect Keith's and Jagg's ascents. The boys were each secured by their own rope and climbed side by side: in time, they arrived at the cave, belay, clothing, helmets and equipment glazed in a veneer of clear ice. Jagg's jacket had kept him dry, but he had a cold pelvis from water running down the rope, something that only leading could change. Keith was wet and toughed it out; everyone laughed at the discomfort.

With the tension cut, we were underway. Keith wasted no time in organizing himself for leading the next pitch. Fearing that inaction would fuse his limbs, he sorted slings and screws with urgency while I tied him into a second rope end. In moments, he was leading. Jagg and I watched in silence as Keith diligently rounded the pillar, his tools loudly smashing the brittle ice at the start of the pitch, the noise dampening as the pillar did. Before long, Keith was ready to belay us up.

With the rope tight to me from above, I had a moment of indecision before my self-discipline voice kicked in. I stripped down to skin, reclaimed my frozen, board-like layers and stretched them over my torso. Then I placed my dry layers in a plastic bag and put them in my pack. The resulting deep chill motivated me to move. Jagg and I climbed side by side, each on our own rope, playfully elbowing each other for the driest line. Climbing next to someone else was fun but distracting. It made the experience less meditative and put my body out of balance, causing me to use more energy. We arrived at the belay, where I changed back into my dry layers, putting my wet clothes in the front of my jacket to keep them from freezing. Looking around from our increasing height, I realized that we were favoured with a fabulous, uncluttered wintery view of the Bow River valley and Banff, beautiful from this position.

Keith and I beamed, having completed our work. It was Jagg's first climb of the season. With his typical defiant ear-to-ear grin, he flippantly shared this detail with us just before starting to lead the last pitch. He looked over his shoulder with a smirk, then left us to ponder as his body seemed to float up the first steep section. The pitch was wet, but not as wet as the others. Jagg moved away swiftly, the sound of his tools declaring the ice conditions good. He expressed his delight while he led, broadcasting, "This is awesome!" I marvelled in surprise at the depth and skill of this man, labelled a ski coach. When he reached the top, a large pumpkin greeted him. On inspection, tacked to the icefall at the top of the climb was a six-foot-diameter oval orange tarp with black felt marker lines – triangle eyes and mouth agape. The day before had been Halloween and the third ascent team had left their mark.

We returned to Banff and continued on to Canmore, to Keith's girlfriend Lisa's house. Lisa was a strong rock climber and understood exactly what our day would entail; she had soup ready for us when we arrived – it was empathy in a bowl. In the morning, still chilled, we went out to the Fireside restaurant in Canmore for a good greasy breakfast to fuel the internal fire. The waitress placed a pitcher of ice water on the table; it sat there a brief while, then in unison, Keith, Jagg and I asked her to "get rid of it" and bring us some hot coffee and tea.

Over the next month and a half, I also climbed The Replicant and Sea of Vapours with other partners. Word had spread about the ease of these famous routes up on Mount Rundle this year, and climbers flocked from all over the world to climb them while they were still in such easy shape.

I felt strong and looked for any opportunity to get out of my valley.

It was early February when I proposed to Keith that we return to Terminator Wall. Still deeply motivated to climb something of significance, I conceived a plan. The natural thing, I suggested to Keith, would be to climb The Replicant and Sea of Vapours, together, along with The Terminator, in one day. I thought that we could minimize the number of changeovers at belays by climbing the routes with a 100-metre rope, twice the typical length. Fewer changeovers would take less time. In all, there would be 450 metres of challenging, technical ice to climb. With a grin, Keith declared his willingness to participate.

I spent a week in Canmore at a friend's place, planning, gathering gear, special-ordering a spool of rope 100 metres long and borrowing Jeff's Grivel ice tools because they were lighter than my Charlet Moser ones.

We camped on the flat alcove that was the typical gear-up spot and I planned to climb The Replicant first because it was straightforward enough to climb in the dark. I would lead 100 metres on The Replicant, and Keith would take the lead on the last fifty metres. Then we would do the same on The Terminator, and finally Keith would lead all of Sea of Vapours.

At 3:00 a.m., we started climbing in the dark; a pool of light illuminated the blue ice before each of us. We ascended the approach pitch again, this time finding ourselves on the ledge below the climbs in moments. I kept up the momentum by stepping directly onto the ice above the snowy shelf and quickly gathered height. The headlamp illuminated both the ice above and down to my feet, but was not strong enough to reveal the gathering void below. This myopic view assisted my psyche and I climbed without hesitation. I now see that the blackness steered me to perceiving myself in a new way.

I eased into a priceless velvet rhythm of climbing; a place of flow an athlete spends a lifetime seeking. The light from the headlamp caused the ice to sparkle in every shade of blue and green imaginable. The focused beam accentuated air pockets, bubbles and hairline fractures as my tool picks displaced the ice during penetration – things I had never seen before in countless daylight pitches. The rhythm of climbing and all that I sensed put me into a kinesthetic meditation; 100 metres of climbing simply disappeared in the blackness that extended below my feet.

I arrived at an ice climber's friend, a small cave formed below a rock overhang in the cliff. The icy vault protects a climber from wind, snow, wetness and the ice that will be falling down when the next person leads. With the sound of a hammer smashing a chandelier, I cleared the icicles around the entrance to make it large enough to enter. Keith was out of the way, so I let ice chunks fall at will. There was an uncharacteristically long silence between my knocking an ice chunk off and the sound of it hitting the ledge below; I played with this effect. Eventually the hole was large enough for me to climb into the cave. I stepped inside and the world changed again. The interior was a harmony of icicles; as the light from my headlamp refracted off them, miniature rainbows danced above me. Unfortunately, I had to clear the icicles hanging from the roof away so that I could stand up in the cave. I swung my ice tool overhead like a vandal shattering fine lead crystal. Once there was sufficient room, I turned around and looked out the entrance. I peered down to the twinkling lights of Banff, while a myriad of stars danced overhead: a surreal nocturnal vision. Banff has always been for adventurer spirits; its streets pulse with the history of people who pushed themselves in harsh environments and those with dreams of challenges to come.

I fashioned a belay anchor and called to a distant Keith to tell him to climb. In response, his beam of light far below slowly got closer. As I reeled in the rope through the belay device and let it gather at my feet, I knew I was experiencing pure magic. The conditions were excellent, it was a beautiful, calm night, and I was warm and comfortable in the midst of a great adventure with a good friend. These thoughts stayed with me the entire time Keith worked to join me. My concerns about the rest of the day were minimal: since we had already climbed The Terminator earlier in the season, the thought of climbing it next was in no way stressful. I knew it would be a challenge, but it would be dry this time.

Keith joined me at the belay, grinning from ear to ear and wearing his 1960s-style thick, horn-rimmed glasses. His headlamp zapped me in the eyes, and I'm sure mine reciprocated. I did not have room for him in my belay cave, so he sorted his equipment outside and shone his lamp and passion off into the darkness above. Having spied a strip of soft, green blue ice that my description had guided his eye to, he said, "I want some of that." He swung a tool and it stuck with the characteristic shudder that speaks volumes to the initiated. We both chuckled like schoolboys. The pitch followed the same tone; a beautiful, surreal, magical playground. We were dancing in the dark.

Nighttime and its curiosities segued into faint light illuminating the Fairholme Range and Cascade Mountain up the Bow Valley. By sunrise we were back down on the ledge below the climbs, in need of a quick rest in preparation to embark on The Terminator. We each guzzled a Boost and sipped a hot drink produced with the stove. I stepped up off the ledge, Keith belaying me with 100 metres of rope stacked neatly at his feet.

I picked my way up the first 50-metre pillar, in similar shape to earlier in the season, but dry. I knew the resting spots, good tool placements and stances for drilling screws. Reaching the first cave belay I carried on without a break. The next fifty metres was steep and required that I read the ice, locate screw placements while minding my body position, and find efficiencies. Against the friction of the rope clipped to fourteen screws, I strained on up to the belay cave, a hundred metres from Keith. As loud as I could, I bellowed "OFF BELAY!!!" so Keith could hear me far below.

A tiny dot started climbing; I relaxed at the belay and let my mind lose focus. It started reeling with excitement, thinking about our success and passing on the story to others. Then I came back to being in the wonderful wild place that is Mount Rundle, to listen to what the situation needed. We were not done yet.

Keith took the lead on the last pitch of The Terminator and I followed, noticing the gathering height below my feet. When rejoined at the top we felt some considerable elation, having ascended two-thirds of the difficulties. We then efficiently rappelled off and down to the ledge.

We warmed and hydrated our bodies with soup and Boost and enjoyed a few moments of inactivity. On the ledge, I was more relaxed than Keith: I was done out front, while his task was leading the entire 150 metres of Sea of Vapours. Once he passed the Postcriptum part of the route, 25 metres up, the ice lost some of its steepness. Within an hour, we were on top.

We hiked down from the climbs, but on our return my perceptions about the purity of what we had accomplished didn't last long; in only a few days' time Guy Lacelle soloed all three routes. Somehow, that announcement destroyed my brilliant memory of what had happened to Keith and me up there. I was back down in the bottom of my valley and once again carried forward the negative. While our ascent was not about my ego while I was up there, it became all about that when I returned to the valley. I quickly forgot how pure my inner voice was while climbing those icy columns, and I descended back into the prison of caring only about what my accomplishments were in the eyes of others. I forgot the beauty of following my own voice: the real practice of climbing and skiing in powerful places. I forgot that self-discovery is all about finding out that the real self lives in the heart, not the head. I had found a green marble on the floor of the ice cave in the middle of the night on The Replicant, but I'd forgotten to save it in my other jar.

CHAPTER 9

LESSON FIVE: PEACE

JULY 1998

With typical climber hauteur, Nancy and I scaled the first obstacle of our day – the chain-link fence that protected the TransAlta hydroelectric dam at Whiteman's Pass above the town of Canmore, Alberta.

The frigid, deep-green reservoir water bubbled against the small concrete dam, further cooling the shady air. The gravel atop the barrier under our feet smelled of earthen lime as we approached Ha Ling Peak, the north face of which towered above us. We had rushed out in the early morning to beat any other climbers to the punch and be the first ones to the route that day.

With 11 long pitches to climb, "it would be a drag to get behind a slow party." I felt the certainty that "other people are the enemy" well up inside me again, as I had done so many times before while trying to "get there first." There had been no other cars in the parking lot. Racing to be the first to the route had become my habit, rationalizing it as somewhat legitimate because rockfall is an issue on some crumbly routes – it puts any second party at great risk. While I'd made a break for the mountains long ago to find peace, I'd brought with me more than just a competitive spirit – I'd also brought a reactive mistrust and judgments about others that I'd cultivated from seed.

Past the dam, and with the same habitual urgency, Nancy set a savage pace up the grade with her strong legs, backpack surging with purpose. Our intent was to climb the north face of Ha Ling Peak, up the bolt-protected sport-climbing route called Sisyphus Summits.

Sisyphus is a character in Greek mythology who gets punished for his disrespect, condemned by Zeus to an eternity of rolling a boulder to the top of a hill. Just below the summit, Sisyphus would always lose control of the massive, cursed stone and it would roll back to the bottom, where he would have to collect it and attempt the task again. Perpetually pushing the rock, Sisyphus lived an existence of eternal frustration from losing control.

The trail led us a short distance through green subalpine fir trees, then onto the open scree and talus above 7,000 feet and treeline. Orange morning light illuminated the summit above us as the sun crested the horizon in the west. Stones grated against each other as I strode atop them, like walking on a freshly gravelled driveway. My legs at once burned and savoured the effort up the steadily inclined path that scored the slope. Ascending, we passed willow, paintbrush, saxifrage, stonecrop, moss campion and bright orange Xanthoria lichen thriving in co-operation with birds, pikas and marmots that live among and on the resource-poor alpine rocks. Our increasing altitude provided views of Canmore, the east end of Mt. Rundle and the dam and lake at Whiteman's Gap, linked to the other features of the landscape by forest under a crystal blue sky. Everything around us was peaceful.

Sweaty effort brought us to the height of land below the towering half-kilometre-high cliff. The ridge in the slope marked the line between shade and sun in the long-shadow morning. The beads of perspiration on my forehead dried on exposure to the sun's rays. I said to Nancy, when I caught up to her at a cairn that marked the base of our intended route, "Here we are! Nice to have no one in front of or behind us."

"It's always worth getting up early ... The route's right here. You can see the line of bolts going across and up," Nancy said as she put on her red helmet.

"Good eye. Wow, that's a lot of bolts!"

It had been a big deal when this route was constructed. First, ascentionists hiked to the top via the tourist trail (like Ha Ling the railway worker himself), but then they rappelled down the steep side with a battery-powered Hilti and drilled two-bolt anchors and protection points on its massive alpine face. That effort had ruffled a few feathers in the climbing community because pre-placed protection, some argued, undermines our respect for and the challenge of a peak – making it a commodity too easily consumed, like everything else. I have revelled equally self-righteously on either side of the bolting argument, whatever supported my ego's immediate interests from time to time. I never openly addressed the merits and challenges of both bolted routes and "clean," leave-no-trace climbing from the ground up, because the assets of each had positively affected me in my own career of ascents. Contradictions continued to exist within me, nurturing conflict.

"I think we should haul your pack. The route traverses enough that any rocks it knocks off won't hit you. It'll make the climbing that much easier. On the less difficult pitches higher up, you can carry it."

"I like that idea," Nancy responded.

We put on our harnesses, laid out the rope, loaded the pack with our runners, rain jackets, water and lunch, then pulled on our rock shoes. I climbed up the grey-black limestone, carefully choosing foot and hand holds, solving the sequences of support the stone presented me, and clipping my rope to the bolt hangers with a quick-draw as I reached them every few metres. The route traversed to the right as much or more than it ascended. I found the intended weakness through the initial overhang and on to the slightly lower-angled rock above. Anchored at the bolted station 25 metres on a diagonal from the ground, I set up to belay Nancy. She climbed up and sideways to join me, and as we readied for the next pitch, two women scrambled up the shady grade and entered the sun on the crest of the slope below. We saw them and I swore under my breath, "Fuck." Recognizing a guide behind us piqued my insecurity, making me now feel I was under scrutiny like the guide candidate I was about to become.

Mounting pressure onto myself, I led off and climbed past the belay station at 25 metres and on to the anchor at the top of pitch three, 50 metres above Nancy. Once secured, I called to Nancy to release the pack, which swung off to climber's right, clear and out of the way. I hauled up on the thin seven-millimetre tag line and, in moments, clipped the pack in. Then I fed the climbing rope through my belay device to protect Nancy while she linked challenging moves and collected the quickdraws from the bolts up the pitch to join me. When she arrived at the fixed point she said, "Those two behind us are obnoxious."

"Oh, yeah?"

"Yes – the guide came right up to me and wanted to clip into the same anchor, which really pissed me off. I made her wait, and said, 'You're moving quickly,' and she replied, 'Yeah, we intend to pass you.' I said, 'Pardon me?' and she repeated, 'We'll be passing you guys.'"

"Just like that?"

"Yes, like she owned the damn place."

"Those fuckin' guides, they think they're God's gift to the mountains!"

"She also said, 'I can't believe you're hauling a pack.'"

"But the route traverses to the right a lot on each pitch," I countered defensively.

"Yeah, you're right, not having the pack worked great and it didn't feel dangerous at all – certainly not to them."

My anxiety about being judged for both our speed and our technique triggered a fit: "There's no fucking way rockfall will be an issue. Those blockheads all think they know what's best. So fucking arrogant. I hate people who try to dictate to me what I can and can't do. We'll see who's fuckin' slow. How many draws do I need on this pitch?"

"Fifteen plus the anchor."

"I'll take 'em all."

My pulse pounded, circulating simmering blood as I clipped quick-draws to my harness gear loops while Nancy passed them to me from hers. Abbreviating my system checks while Nancy tried to keep things safe, I launched from the security of the bolted station and started our third pitch with something to prove. Fuelled by hate, I raced up the stone. A few metres above the belay was a crux section of smooth, 75-degree stone with hand- and footholds the width of the top of a light-switch plate. I scaled that rock like a baboon escaping up a tree away from the jaws of a predator, pasting my black shoes on the tiny edges and stepping up to the larger holds above. I clipped into and climbed past the midpoint anchor at 25 metres, then moved diagonally up and right for the same distance to a good ledge and another belay station. The pitch took only minutes to lead and I secured myself to the bolts with a sling, carabiners and rope. My right biceps burned while I speed-hauled the pack without stone fall.

Nancy climbed the polished slab with ease. Reaching the belay, she said, "That was fun, especially since I didn't have the pack on. I think we can relax now that we're ahead of them."

Not responding to her, I organized myself for the fourth lead. The prickly rillenkarren (water-worn) limestone made dashing up the "black book" feature easy, pulling on sharp handholds and effortlessly reading moves. Fury-nourished, I was surprised to see that my climbing was devoid of its usual hesitation. My single purpose was to be as far ahead of the other team as possible by the end of the climb. Everything else disappeared; my need to prove myself was paramount. Our position was stunning, it was a blue-sky day and our vista stretched down the Bow Valley all the way to Canmore, but it was peripheral to my experience and I saw nothing of it. When I clipped myself in, the pair in question clung to the face 100 metres below me, starting the difficult slab pitch.

I tagged the pack up, clipped it to the bolts and pulled hard on the orange rope through the belay device in an attempt to speed Nancy's ascent. The rope moved more slowly than I wanted, but eventually we both hung from the pair of bolts 175 metres off the ground.

On reaching me, Nancy said, "Don't pull so hard on

the rope, it knocks me off balance. Keep me tight but don't pull."

I grunted a dispassionate, "Sorry!"

Far below, we saw a member of the party behind flailing on the crux section on the third pitch. They struggled and fell repeatedly on the smooth slab while wearing their large packs. I said to Nancy, "Look at those idiots; they're gonna pass me – like hell. I'm gonna frickin' dust 'em." Turning my attention to the climbing ahead, I commented, "This notch above us looks difficult."

"Yeah, this pitch is supposed to be one of the harder ones on the route. You should take your time with it."

Ignoring Nancy, I maniacally rushed everything, mumbling "we intend to pass you" to fuel myself. The moves the pitch demanded of me were challenging. I responded like a man possessed, thinking little of safety. My right foot popped off a hold 180 metres off the ground, I was nearly in the air, but caught myself before I fully peeled off. Regaining composure, I pulled the moves with greater ease and raced up to the belay station.

When Nancy reached my fixed point, she said, "I can't believe it! You flew up that and it was hard climbing. But you can probably slow down now; we have a good lead on them."

"I'm not slowing down. They need humbling."

I rushed up the next pitch. From my anchor, I could no longer see the pair behind us, long gone now, alone on the steeper face below. Nancy and I rejoined and I said to her, "Can you wear the pack now that it's easier and straight up?"

"Yeah, I can do that. Are you gonna ease up?"

"Nope. I don't wanna see those two again."

"Ken, you don't need to rush."

"Nobody labels ME as SLOW, Nance!"

Nancy shrank back, hanging on the anchor with a countenance of disbelief as I remained single-minded.

The rope trailing behind, I padded up the slabby pitch in perpetual motion, lunging for holds and clipping bolts in my Sisyphean effort. When we negotiated the final steep section, the following party was nowhere in sight. I held the rope to protect Nancy up the last pitch to the summit.

With the afternoon light on the south-facing gentle grade at the top, we untied from the rope and coiled it, took off our harnesses, ate fruitcake and loaded our one pack. I gloated over our fast ascent. Standing near the edge of the cliff at the climb's summit like the Grinch glowering down at Whoville, I spoke into the void below me as the wind came up the face to meet my words and shouted, "Pass us, eh? Not likely, fuckers!"

On our descent of the easy scree-slopes dotted with wind-stunted conifers, I continued my complaints about the arrogance of mountain guides – how I hated their ego-based approach while bemoaning the prospect of my rock-climbing exam in September. Nancy, supportive and tactful as always, told me that she was impressed at how fast I climbed. I was not mature enough to hear her say that I had scared her, compromising safety for speed. I had once again lost control of my Sisyphean boulder, and it rolled back to the bottom, priming me for another fruitless effort. We arrived at the parking lot and loaded the gear into our blue Mazda pickup, while I continued to stew in the day's drama.

> "We see the world, not as it is, but as we are or as we are conditioned to see it."
>
> —Steven Covey[10]

My penchant for demonizing others had become a part of my approach to the mountains from early on. The drama and conflict I generated internally and unconsciously at times became more important than safety when I let others push my insecurity buttons. Insane rage too often usurped magic, beauty and peace, all well within my grasp but usually light years from my awareness. I found an orange marble at the first belay station on Sisyphus summit, in the recognition that peace begins with me and deeply affects the safety of myself and others in hazardous environments.

The guide behind us, as it turned out, was Diny Harrison, who was very helpful the summer after the avalanche. Out of the blue, she called me up and made sure I was out climbing, to help me to continue to feel part of the guiding community and get me back on the horse. I am grateful to her and marvel at what a good person she is as I put that orange marble into my other jar.

CHAPTER 10

LESSON SIX: ACTING ON INTUITION

AUGUST 1999

The process of becoming a mountain guide was a love–hate experience for me. I love the mountains, and my dream of making a living in them was strong. On the other hand, I loathe tests, especially in a hazardous environment where my tolerance for risk is seemingly no longer under my control. I battled with staying true to my approach to the mountains during the training courses because in my recreational climbing, I had usually turned around whenever I had a bad "feeling." So far, the practice had served me well. In 1999 it was put to the test.

Official decision-making protocols on one particular exam left me with the distinct impression that the assessment of candidates in the course leaned toward being a cookie-cutter process. Students' actions needed to be in line with what the examiner thought should happen – if they were not they were automatically categorized as "out in left field." Intuition often gets a bad rap in a world dominated by the idea that everything is quantifiable. Not many people are exact gingerbread men, so the failure rate for candidates on exams for many years through the 1990s was 50 per cent or higher.

In 1998, after fifteen years of climbing and a five-year career teaching outdoor pursuits at Mount Royal College in Calgary, I embarked on the process of becoming a certified guide. In the process I learned a great deal about guiding, and I value those lessons. But it was also a training and apprenticeship that nearly killed me on two occasions. Worse, it caused me to abandon my own sense of what was right in order to fit in and become one of their gingerbread men.

Along with the application requirements and ancillary prerequisites for becoming a mountain guide, candidates are required to demonstrate proficiency and technical leadership ability in rock climbing, alpine climbing and ski touring, at two levels. First, one has to achieve an "assistant" level, which leads to a one- or two-year apprenticeship under supervision of a mountain guide before taking the full guide examinations, with one exception: in the full guide stream, one can skip the top level Rock Guide course/exam because those skills are covered in the top level Alpine Guide exam. The Rock Guide certification exists for people who wish to work only in rock terrain.

After great success with my assistant (apprentice) rock

and ski exams, I was on cloud nine in early 1999. My evaluations were glowing, with comments like "great job, Ken, demonstrated a benchmark standard," and "your mountain experience is apparent." I was ticking through the credentials quickly and seemed to have found my niche. By the summer of that year I embarked on my last assistant (apprentice) level exam, aiming to complete all three disciplines to apprenticeship levels within a year. I had my sights on being a full guide in three or four years.

At the time, the Assistant Alpine exam was two weeks long. The conditions in the Rockies were excellent, providing dry rock and good alpine ice and snow. The weather was stunning, with clear blue skies for both weeks. We climbed many of the classics in the Canadian Rockies: in the Bow Valley on alpine rock objectives like Mt. Louis, Castle Mountain, Mt. Cory, Mt. Ball and Mt. Bell; at the Columbia Icefield on the big alpine ice faces of Mt. Athabasca and Mt. Andromeda; and in the Lake Louise group on Mt. Victoria, Mt. Lefroy and Mt. Aberdeen for overall alpine experiences on mixed ice and rock. All of the objectives are peaks that clients typically aspire to climb on a two-week climbing holiday.

Examiners assessed our client care, risk management, technical systems for climbing, glacier travel, professionalism, mountain movement skills, instructional technique and mountain sense. Each night, examiners presented candidates with an intended route on a mountain for the next day, on which they were to be tested. This method of withholding the objective until the night before prevented the aspirant guides from practising the routes weeks beforehand, and therefore allowed an evaluation of the examinees' ability to guide on sight, navigate, read terrain efficiently and make competent intellectual decisions based on the current conditions. It was a seemingly complete approach from the perspective of quantifiable information-gathering and technical application in and of the assessment of the candidates' skills. But guiding in hazardous environments also must be an intuitive process because of the complexity of the ever-changing conditions and circumstances in the mountains and within groups.

On a guide's course, candidates were typically grouped in threes, with one examiner. This allowed the assessor to see all elements of the lead candidate's performance and watch the other two, who were working behind in a guide-client rope team, from a distance. Candidates rotated into each position throughout the course of a day, acting as lead guide for the examiner, as assistant guide leading the second rope, and as the client in the second party. Only the examiner was in the role of a client all day; however, he or she had a very difficult and dangerous assignment. They tied in with a candidate and observed them performing their tasks undisturbed, yet needed to "step in" the moment before a terrible mistake. Step in too soon, before a critical action, and the candidate could become frustrated. Step in too late, and it could cost a life. This scenario was a difficult tightrope walk to negotiate for each assessor. It required heavy use of intuition, but this critical tacit application of a skill was not imparted to the candidates.

There are two agendas governing any mountain guide exam. The first is to assess standard guiding practice for typical objectives on rock, snow and ice and in alpine environments, noting how the candidate manages the "expected" in a typical guiding situation. The second agenda relates to the idea that in the mountains, anything can happen. Candidates are required to react to the unexpected so an evaluation can occur of how they manage dynamic mountain situations. Sometimes this is a real-life challenge that the mountains deliver; at other times the candidates respond to an artificial scenario conjured up by the examiner.

One hazard I encountered more than once during my Assistant Guide course was the cultural assumption that the examiner has enough experience to use instinct, but the guide candidate does not. This presumption is based on a belief that the development of any so-called "sixth sense" is the result of experience and therefore should be part of a rational process based on years of decision-making in the mountains. I eventually allowed myself to be indoctrinated into this dogmatic belief. But like nearly everything in life, intuition is much more mysterious and multi-faceted in its true nature.

On day four of the 1999 Assistant Alpine Guide exam, while driving home after climbing Mt. Louis, I answered a cellphone call from Bill, who was the course leader of a team of three examiners and a guide who lived in Canmore. As I listened to him while driving down the road in the passenger seat of an old Toyota 4Runner, he said, "You, Adam and Mark, a friend of mine who will be a volunteer client, are going to climb Castle Tower by the normal route on the east face tomorrow. From the summit, I want you to descend the west face to a notch between Castle Tower and the rest of Castle Mountain. You've had a long day on Mt. Louis today, and this descent will make it easier because we can short-rope our way down."

Short-roping is a way of a group moving, roped together, with less rope out to improve communication and control between them, and using naturally occurring anchors rather than placed ones. It tends to be quick because generally all parties are moving at the same time and relying on rock features and simple rope-work to protect the climbers from a slip that could lead to a fall.

I stiffened, instantly recognizing that this was a poor choice, especially if the intent was to make the descent less demanding. I had climbed and descended the route earlier in the summer and there was a different way to get down easily. When I questioned him, saying, "That doesn't sound easier," he replied, "Oh, it's gonna be easier!"

That evening during my preparations in Canmore, while carbo-loading at a friend's house, I made several calls to local guides to gather information about the proposed west face way down. Every guide I contacted said that it was going to be dangerous, noting that there would be a lot of loose rock since the cliff had not seen much traffic lately to clean it. One of the guides I called that evening said, "Boy, that descent route sounds like contrived guide's course bullshit." That night I also got a call from another friend, Geoff Creighton, who decided to leave the exam. He told me he was pulling out after having a rough day; the news was difficult because of the respect I had for his ability.

The next morning, four of us collected in the black pre-dawn at Castle Mountain parking lot as Adam, Mark, Bill and I circled around, headlamps illuminating the packs on the gravel. Adam had been a former student of mine at Mount Royal College – he was a stronger climber than I was, having climbed to a higher standard on rock. Our relationship was now different, with both of us being candidates; I felt a little insecure about him seeing a different, more vulnerable, side of me. Mark was a friend of Bill's, whom Bill had enlisted to come and be "the client" for a day.

After exchanging good mornings, I addressed Bill respectfully about the line of descent, saying, "I called several guides last night and they all said the same thing: that descending the west face to the notch is not a good idea, especially if the goal is to be easier and quicker." Adam kicked at the gravel awaiting Bill's response, seeming nervous but happy that I had broached the question; Mark seemed indifferent.

As if a burr had been lodged between his skin and

backpack, Bill responded, "My wife did it with another guide years ago, and it goes."

Not feeling heard, I added, "One of the people I called even said, 'That descent route sounds like contrived guide's course bullshit.'"

Bill smiled uncomfortably but was not willing to adjust the itinerary. Irritated that I had such little control entering into this hazardous situation, I put my gut feeling aside and led our hike through the dark Engelmann spruce forest, up the treed base of the mountain to the rock towers above.

At first light, we reached the upper mountain headwall; the rising sun cast a gorgeous pink luminosity on the climbing route. Below and to the south the terrain opened to a beautiful alpine meadow that the early morning light skipped across like a smooth pebble on the surface of a calm pond. With much better care than we'd spent on the development of our social environment, we checked one another's harnesses and tie-in points to the rope before our hands touched the rock. In two groups of two, we short-roped up the initial rock steps. I led Mark on the second rope team while Adam led Bill out front, finding the way. We moved easily up the broken terrain and gullies with simple belay stances and use of terrain to protect our progress, ascending to a massive ledge that wraps around the whole mountain.

After hiking up the slope of the ledge, Adam and Bill negotiated the Dragon's Back and the difficult move out of the notch, staying in the lead for two more pitches.

Then I tied in with Bill, understanding that I would lead to the summit. Placing pieces of gear in the cracks and clipping the rope to them for protection as I went, I climbed short pitches to facilitate communication while belaying "my client" up to each anchor station. The climbing was easy, so we made rapid progress and reached the summit before midday. This is the easy part of guiding – managing the technical systems – but the whole day my gut roiled about our descent plans and the conflict we'd had about them.

The flat, expansive limestone of the mountaintop allowed us to walk up and over the summit with "our hands in our pockets," enjoying endless views of craggy peaks through a slight summer haze that hinted of fires somewhere in British Columbia. The giant U-shaped valley below us to the south stretched all the way to Lake Louise in the west and past Canmore in the east. We traversed across to the top and west side of the proposed descent route.

There we had a snack and water as we transitioned from the stroll across the peak to technical descent mode. Adam took over the lead again for our way down and began organizing ropes while I peered down the west face, munching on my granola bar. It was immediately apparent to me that my research was reliable; this would be an involved and dangerous descent. What I saw before us was a steep limestone cliff with loose rock balanced precariously on countless small ledges. Instead of scrambling down easy, stepped-rock terrain, we would have to leave equipment fixed in the rock, anchor our ropes and rappel. I said again, "This doesn't look like easy short-roping."

Bill stiffened with a defiant self-righteous smirk and said, "Let's go see," now ambiguous about abandoning the idea of a simple descent but saying nothing to clearly communicate the change in plan, if there was one.

With all of the rope systems ready for a technical descent, Adam lowered me first with the intent of removing poised loose rock by trundling it off the cliff so it would not be teetering above our heads once we were exposed on the face. "Lowering" meant that no equipment was to be below me, to reduce the chances of anything getting damaged by any of the rock I pushed off. As I cleared tottering piles of limestone off the ledges, the effort was a clear indication of the danger that was to follow. Once on a ledge below, I stood there feeling powerless to stop the extreme risk from continuing, but on a faint level I recognized that I feared failing the exam more than I feared the danger.

Mark descended next, then Bill, before Adam followed. My voice inside said, "This is a bad place, Ken," as I watched each of them gingerly descend, hoping no additional loose rock they disturbed would fall on the ledge where I stood. As each in turn arrived on the stance, I anchored and instructed them to hide under an overhang of rock on climber's left. Once standing on the large ledge at the bottom, Adam divided the two strands of rope and pulled the blue one. As the blue rope piled at his feet, the green rope ascended the cliff, sliding through the top anchor. When the end of the rope fell from above, it brought with it a shower of loose stones. The four of us cowered under the overhang, fortunate that no rock big enough to cause harm came down. With the rope now at our feet on the loose cobble ledge, we felt committed. I joked, "Well it looks like we can still climb out of here. But it does not look easy or fun."

Adam looked stressed in the lead and I could see on his face that he agreed with my assessment about our route. But he said nothing, straining to manage loose rock on each leg of our descent, knocking the worst bits off from above, positioning the team and being vigilant. He worked hard to find solid anchors; good cracks, large boulders or horns from which to create fixed points for our journey down the rubble-strewn wall. Because it was so difficult, the necessary personal stake we all had in securing ourselves led to a breakdown in the exam scenario. Everyone scanned the rock walls looking for cracks in solid rock to hammer in our pitons, and secure all of us. Three of us were moving around unclipped from any system from time to time, searching for any way to anchor ourselves in the shattered terrain. The tone became more like a common adventure than a guide's exam, in some small part because of Adam's leadership, but mostly because of the demands of the situation on all of us to assume responsibility for ourselves. From time to time Bill would remember that this was supposed to be an exam, and required us to play our "roles." This breakdown of the lesson's structure made me wonder why we were putting ourselves at such risk. Back in the assistant guide role, on the fourth rappel, Adam lowered me down to find a place to stage the last rappel to the notch. After lowering 48 metres, I called up for him to stop. I took my pack off and placed it on an end-table-sized ledge to access more rock-climbing hardware. With Adam waiting to lower Mark down on the second rope, I felt rushed to get an anchor prepared. I did more rope-less scrambling around and was able to get a one-nut anchor into a tapering crack in the rock and clip the end of the rope to it. I attached myself to the J that this created in the rope extending from the top anchor where Bill, Adam and Mark were standing all the way down to my nut. Once ready, Adam lowered Mark, whom I clipped into the nut and rope when he arrived. Mark spoke to me after he arrived at the stance; until that moment he had held his cards close. "This is not what I expected," he said.

Feeling like a victim, I replied, "It *is* the epic *I* expected. I had a bad feeling about this from the start, and I confirmed it with research, but that seems to mean nothing here."

We gave each other a knowing glance and I moved back to the small ledge on the left where my pack was sitting, because there was not enough room on his ledge to stand beside him. Without warning, the three-foot-square shelf I was standing on gave way. I fell ten feet before my J system came tight. Rock and debris showered down the canyon between Castle Tower and the rest of Castle Mountain, echoing with booms and bashes as microwave-oven-size blocks bounced down the face and hit the ground below. With the rock went my blue "Wild Things" pack, and all of my gear went clattering down the cliff with it. I hung from the rope for a moment in shock before I Batmanned back up to Mark.

With eyes the size of saucers, Mark whispered as I stood next to him on his tiny ledge, "Holy shit, Ken, I've never seen a ledge collapse before."

Bill rappelled down the ropes above to join us, and when he was within earshot I said, "Nice quick, easy descent-route, Bill!" He said nothing; even while I shared my story of the ledge collapse, he kept an expressionless face as he switched me to the lead guide for the last pitch down.

I found and built a piton anchor once I had gathered some equipment from Adam and we descended safely down to the notch. Grudgingly, I picked up my scattered belongings, including the bits of cellphone to reassemble. I also rallied my composure for the short-rope down the gully to the path and on to the car.

Bill steered clear of any discussion about the choice of route and how it related to his stated goal of having a day with an easy descent. What we needed to talk about was avoided and I did not broach it, having said it all on the mountain. I also did not share the detail of my being unclipped just before the ledge collapse, for fear that I would fail my exam, even though Bill had modelled unroped climbing and neither the route nor the technique had been appropriate for the terrain – all of it had been ego-based and not inherently necessary. At day's end, I vowed to take stronger action if ever again I became uncomfortable with the objectives of an exam. I clearly saw my near miss as a warning: I needed to follow my own sense of what was right more closely.

Eight days later, after a busy journey to the Columbia Icefield, on day 12 of the 14-day assessment, my group of candidates teamed up with Karl Nagy as our examiner. Karl was a wonderful man who deeply understood the mountains. Burly, intelligent, but most importantly humble, Karl was willing to listen to candidates, and because of this attribute he was well-liked and respected. While among the most competent of any of the examining team, he was nevertheless new to the assessment process.

Our candidate group comprised Jason, Kent and myself. Karl gave us good, solid information for the upcoming day; our objective was the north peak of Mt. Victoria in the Lake Louise group. The route was to hike along the west shore of Lake Louise up to the Plain of Six Glaciers Teahouse, then ascend the upper Victoria Glacier to the col between the north peak of Victoria and Mt. Collier. Once there, the objective was to climb Mt. Victoria's northeast ridge. My task for the day was to lead the leg from the summit of Mt. Victoria back to the col between it and Collier, which I considered an easy leg.

We left the Lake Louise parking lot at 3:00 a.m., guided by the light from our headlamps and the stars. After we ambled along the cool, flat path to the back of the lake, our journey went uphill to the upper Victoria Glacier. At dawn the sky was so clear that everything sparkled in vibrant colour en route to the ice. At the sunny, warm toe of the glacier, we enjoyed a novel view of Abbot Pass and the stone hut there, while drinking water and munching on snacks. As we put on our harnesses, I noticed how tired everyone looked. Jason was sick with a chest cold and had a terrible, hacking cough. Kent's body language indicated he was weary, and Karl, known for his endurance, lay down for a quick nap during the break. I was as tired as anyone and had a bad feeling about our situation. There was a tension in the air because no one was willing to be honest about energy levels. Fatigue meant that we would not be as sharp or as safe as we should be for alpine climbing. An honest appraisal of this fact would be part of any solid mountain-guiding decision-making process. Unless, of course, the intent of the day was to assess our ability to climb as safely as we were able while fatigued. But nobody addressed this.

Tied into the rope with ten-metre spacing we trod on up the glacier and I continued to observe sluggish body language by everyone. Since I was playing the role of the client, at the back of the group, the unstated rule was that it was not my place to confront what might be going on; the role of the client during exams was strictly to follow and let things unfold, only giving an opinion when asked. Weary of "the game," and feeling like this was a recipe for disaster, I took matters into my own hands.

I checked in with Jason, using him as a sounding board and perception test, and he clearly said that he was feeling poorly. I asked him if he would stick by me if I called the day off and he reticently said he would.

Immediately after checking with him, I called the group together on the glacier. The terrain required that we remain roped up; walking on the glacier alone would not be prudent. This meant that if I went down, everyone had to come. In light of this fact and my experiences earlier in the exam, I said, "This is not the start of some discussion that goes around in circles and then we continue on with the climb. We are going down from here." My language was strong because I wanted to act on what I felt in my heart. When finished, I felt the kind of relief that comes from telling the truth. I felt like a man for once, willing to say what I believe, regardless of the consequences.

Karl stood there with his mouth hanging open, not knowing what to do or say. He made a suggestion to change the objective, but I said, "This group is not fit for technical terrain today." Respectfully, Karl listened to my assessment then challenged us with some navigation exercises, including a resection to find our exact location. An hour later we descended the glacier and were back at the Alpine Club of Canada hostel in Lake Louise by 1:00 p.m.

When the other groups came back from their objectives, I felt my action validated. The results of the day among the other groups were abysmal. People had made all kinds of mistakes and paid for it with their grades. There were some failures and numerous marginal performances. Still, some of the candidates made fun of how I had conducted my day.

After everyone had showers, and before the next day's objectives were announced, Bill took me aside. Standing next to the pine railing on the front deck of the hostel, he said, "What the heck were you doing out there today?"

"I saw that people were tired and had a strange feeling about it. This time I needed to correct the situation before anyone was hurt."

"But that's not your call to make," he said. "That was Karl's call, and he didn't seem to think anything was a problem. I also checked in with the others in your group and they all said they were fine. I have to take this as a fitness issue for you."

Feeling betrayed by Jason because he had given me his word that he would stand by me, I protested: "What I saw was weariness among all of us, and I had a bad feeling about any of us making good decisions on the mountain today."

"I don't know about that. I'll have to bring this

situation up with the technical committee. I'll call them all tonight and collectively they'll decide what to do."

I felt incredibly alone and frustrated that nobody had the courage to validate any of my perceptions, especially Jason, who had said he would. However, I chose not to confront him because I thought it would only lead to an argument. It felt like everyone was watching out for their own interests only as they related to the exam, perhaps even Karl. I wrestled with the notion that maybe I was the problem, but when I considered the situation rationally, I became even more angry at the system.

My future as a candidate was placed in limbo while the technical committee deliberated about whether I still met the course requirements. Still, the assessment carried on the next day and we climbed a shoulder of Mt. Bell. Tasked with finding the easiest descent, I kept my eyes peeled while ascending and spotted a walk-off. During my lead, I short-roped for a few minutes until I found my series of simple benches to the bottom. It was so easy that Bill said, astonishingly, "That was too easy."

"You tasked me with getting down the easiest way and I did that," I replied. He didn't answer.

That evening, I met with Bill again to discuss the situation. He said, "The technical committee determined that you need to complete an extra day at the end of the week, with Karl on Mt. Aberdeen. You'll climb the glacier route to the Aberdeen–Haddo col and return home after that."

"So I'm being punished?" I asked, thinking both Karl

and I were being penalized: I for mutiny, he for allowing it.

"Think of it as an opportunity to succeed and complete the course. They could have recommended failure."

Reluctant, I said, "Okay."

Even though that extra day was beautiful, I remained focused on being embarrassed that I was still on the course while my contemporaries were done. I resented what seemed to me a punishment. Karl seemed different too. We had good conversations about climbing and the mountains, but I sensed an edge to him that I had never noticed before. I guided him up Aberdeen Glacier – easy travel with a couple of pitches of ice climbing under beautiful clear skies.

At the rocky flats between Aberdeen and Haddo, surrounded by magnificent snow-covered peaks, Karl and I talked about the assessment.

He said, "Good job leading up here. We examiners wanted to share some things with you about your assessment."

"Okay."

Looking at his field book, he said, "Keep developing your short-roping skills."

"Yeah, that one is always on the list."

"Yes, short-roping takes a while to master and it just needs miles."

"Yup."

"We think you need to work on differentiating between real risk and perceived risk."

"You know, Karl, I made my decision based on what I felt and what I saw. That is all I can do."

"I don't want to get into a big debate here, but I need to say that we feel like your assessments at times seemed 'from left field.'"

"Okay, what else?" I said, feeling pissed off, defensive and sensing a change in Karl.

"Keep working on your endurance. It seems like you did not have enough in you and that led to your decision on Victoria."

"I have a different version of that story."

"Yes, it appears that you do, but just remember, you were given the opportunity to pass by the committee, Ken."

"But nobody is telling me that good guiding also requires knowing when to turn around."

"At this point in your guiding career that responsibility is exclusively the supervising guide's. Incidentally, under the Mountain Sense category it says here, 'You exhibit good judgment.'"

Angered, I heard but did not internalize the last comment. Still, I mustered a "thanks, Karl."

He said, "Congratulations, you passed."

We took the rope off and quickly climbed, unroped, down the backside of Haddo Peak, then proceeded around to the pass between Fairview and Saddleback mountains, then down the path to the car. When we returned to the hostel I learned that at least half of the candidates had failed.

Adam had failed. I learned from him that his high level of ability on rock actually affected his route-finding assessment negatively. The examiners thought he chose lines that seemed too difficult, instead of looking around the corner for the easy way. Adam never returned to do another course or exam. His promising career as a guide was over before it had begun. I could not help but think that there are countless ways up or down a mountain and that, especially in Adam's case, some of the examiners had been wrong to only accept one way. It seems as though a broader picture is elusive in the assessment of people, and not only in the guiding life. I felt fortunate to have passed, but carried forward a great deal of bitterness about how I and others had been treated.

In 2000, the next year, Karl was working as an examiner on the Assistant Alpine exam, and again he faced candidates who wanted to turn around, this time because they were in terribly bad weather. Their objective for the day had been to climb the north face of Mt. Fay. Over lunch inside the Neil Colgan hut, they decided to change their goal to Mt. Little because of the conditions. En route to Mt. Little, the candidates asked again to turn around and head home. Karl refused, wanting to make better use of the day, so they kept going into the wind, snow and mist. As they approached the cliffs of Mt. Little, a large block of rock came hurtling out of the fog and hit Karl directly in the head. He died of his injuries as shocked candidates continued their efforts to save his life. His death left a hole in the world, his new wife a widow, candidates traumatized and a gap in the guiding community.

I learned the wrong lesson from my experience in 1999; I became a sheep, willing to follow without listening to or acting on my own intuition. The fear of being punished again for using my intuition further nourished my integration into a stubborn, deadly hierarchy. Karl's death should have been validation enough for me to know my actions were true and I was on track, but it wasn't. I had sought validation for my ability to accurately judge situations in the mountains from the examining team, which I never got. But carrying the right lesson forward from this disappointment was ultimately my responsibility.

The only unofficial recommendation to come from Karl's death was to make sure everyone in a group knows how to use the guide's radio. The candidates on the day of his death did not know how Karl's radio worked, which drastically complicated the rescue. There were no further recommendations, nor was there an inquiry.

Acting on intuition is critical and requires a large measure of social courage; the mysterious quality of the sixth sense is sometimes at odds with our science- and technology-shaped minds. It is a gut feeling that is neither measurable nor quantifiable in any way, nor is its source identifiable. It comes "from left field." In most social environments, we are required to have a rational argument for our actions, and gut feelings are not a result of rational thinking. But in fact, analytical thought often gets in the way of hearing intuitive information; it is the noise that keeps us from hearing the kind of information we most need at the time. While carefully processed experience may be an aid to developing good intuition, it is not the only important variable. We must also listen to our inner guidance system and have the courage to act on it.

I found a dark blue marble in my memory of standing in a circle on the upper Victoria Glacier, speaking my truth, knowing it to be valid, and placed it in my other jar.

CHAPTER 11

LESSON SEVEN: TRUTH

"All that is transitory is but metaphor."

—Goethe

Mike Stack steers the silver 15-passenger Dodge van into the Galatea parking lot, in Kananaskis Country, Alberta. It is a beautiful warm late July day in 1984. The aspen leaves have reached their mature dark green. They sound like someone playing a rain stick as a gentle breeze dances through them. The soothing sound floods the van as it stops. Outside, to the north, Mt. Kidd's towering grey limestone walls loom 3,000 feet above our heads to the north. Eight thirteen-year-old boys, carried by disproportionately long legs, tumble out the side door and extract their overstuffed aluminum-frame packs from the back of the van. This five-day trip will make up a good portion of their two-week session at Camp Chief Hector. We do a teaching segment on managing blisters. Jim Buckton and I check pack straps and belts. Then the ten of us shoulder our loads and start connecting boots with the Galatea Lakes trail. An image of Lillian Lake's green waters, carried in our mind's eye, makes the loads on our backs seem lighter.

Initially the path leads downhill. It is edged with kinnikinnik, trembling aspen, Engelmann spruce and lodgepole and Jack pine. The air is a mix of all of them, stirred by air rising from the sun-warmed ground we walk upon. At the hill's bottom the track crosses the clear blue waters of the Kananaskis river on a suspension bridge. The trail, at times rocky, winds its way up the forested valley. Alongside, Galatea Creek is filled with the cool, fresh smell and roaring sound of water cascading over rocks. The look on the young faces tells a story of struggle, tenacity, discomfort, strength, uncertainty and wonder. Every bit of this is good. At a bridged creek crossing, having put several kilometres behind us, we take off our loads to lunch. We drink in a view brimmed with a wooded landscape carpeted in rich green moss right up to creek's edge. Each of us takes stock of the beauty in which we are engulfed, yet we are foiled by the inability of words to capture and contain the allure of our surroundings.

Stoned wheat thins, cheese, salami and several handfuls of trail mix fuel us for the second half of our journey. Jim and I monitor the boys to be sure they play prudently. We talk about *Ghostbusters*, Gretzky and the Stanley Cup, and of course the greatness of eating pizza. Our conversation is trite compared to how most of us feel about being here in this mountain valley. Chatting carries us away from the "Now." We know we are being distracted but make small talk anyhow. We relax under the cool forest canopy for over an hour. A chill creeps into our bodies from the heat stolen from sweat evaporating off our damp T shirts. We need to move. I bark, "Okay, boys, let's load up." Reticently, we pick up our packs (some awkwardly), wobble them into position on our backs and thread webbing through our steel waist buckles. We only carry things that either sustain or protect us. Knowing that what we carry is useful, the burden is easier to bear.

The trail steepens. It opens to the sky as it crosses avalanche paths blasted by snow and cleared of rigid-trunked aspens and conifers. In their place alders now grow, flexible enough to bend to the power of avalanches that roar down these slopes each winter.

We holler and whistle one at a time, the sound we make intended to warn bears that could be foraging on berries that grow in these open glades. We hope our noise alerts lurking omnivores to our presence, and hope they move on without being surprised and scared into defending themselves. Fear is the root of violence in all mammals.

With sore shoulders, hips and feet, and in deep anticipation of putting our loads down, we trudge along the north side of Lillian Lake's green waters. Happily we find good camping in a stand of old Engelmann spruce, along the west shore. Jim takes off his pack, pulls out his sleeping mat, and then sits and leans against a mature tree, confident the boys will remain close to him. He is right.

With tarps set and food stowed, the boys wander around the lake, many with a stick in hand. When we all take a dip in the frigid snowmelt water, the hoots and yells echo off a distant cliff.

After swimming, one of the boys picks up a stone and skips it, and we are all on to a new game. For the next hour we skip stones across the lake's smooth surface. The goal is to get the stone to bounce clear across the water and land on the moss and heather on the other side. There are two games, really: first, to find the best flat, rounded stones, and then to spin them out low over the water at just the perfect angle so they bounce the most times. The highest skip count was over a dozen.

Arms now sore, we head back to our camp, spark up the Coleman "Peak 1" stove and boil a big pot of water. After a dinner of egg noodles, tuna and orange cheese powder, we turn in for a night's sleep. I crawl into my new red sleeping bag atop my blue closed-cell foam pad and drift off, surrounded by the vast power that is the mountains.

I rise early the next morning, make a mug of coffee, and walk down to the lakeshore. Everyone else is still asleep. The calm waters reflect Mt. Kidd's south peak in a perfect mirror image. The stillness comforts and calms me. I sit on a sun-bleached log in complete silence. The image of the mountain reflected on the water is translucent, so I can also see submerged, silt-covered rocks and logs. I can feel myself both reflected and at depth. Mirrored, I see the emptiness I carry inside. The emptiness I almost always try to remedy by seeking more. More attention, more accomplishments, more everything. I also feel I am being held by nature, and that by being still I can access the feeling of belonging I've always craved. Palpable also is the knowledge that I have joined the generations before me in knowing that the solutions to life's challenges exist in nature, which is also deep within myself. The lesson is implicit, begging to become a daily practice. The whispered message is that truth comes from silence rather than action.

The coolness of the morning is warmed by the sun that advances up the sky above the ridge to the east. With the elevation of the brilliant rays, my contemplative morning dissolves. Sounds come from camp. I grab my empty cup and rush off to make oatmeal. Our plan for the day is to hike up to Guinn's Pass. Gotta keep the boys busy, I think to myself. My moment of insight is gone.

Busy would become my life for the next twenty years. I rushed from one adventure event to the next, searching for something I could have found by sitting next to a calm lake. Like the skipping-stones of the boys at Lillian Lake, I would skim along the surface of events in my life, never slowing down enough to sink into the depths and harvest any real meaning. In my haste to fill my days, I missed what life itself was meant to teach me. A practice of maturing into greater awareness, and taking bold action on what I knew to be right for me. The most hazardous part of this game of adventure has been taking unconscious action. My rhetoric around the value of adventure was about facing down fear. However, being an adventurer was the best place to hide for someone as socially timid as myself. I was camouflaged by the illusion of physical courage I projected. But I never took courageous social action in situations that called for it. My fear of looking at myself – and learning how I was showing up in my life – had grave consequences for those I was meant to take care of on Tumbledown. Stillness terrified me. Without distraction, I could see all of the things about my behaviour that were painful to see. Looking away seemed to be a remedy but made it worse because consequence grew. Had I stopped for long enough, I would have seen that many of my actions were what a boy would do, not a man. That morning at Lillian Lake I left behind the truth I learned about stillness. The marble sat on the sun-bleached log by the lake's edge.

However, whispers from that edge have always stayed with me. But they were like a recurring dream that depicts a lesson one never quite takes the time to understand. The whispers were with me the morning of the La Traviata avalanche tragedy. The lake I pictured myself sitting next to in peace and freedom was my memory of that morning at Lillian Lake. My higher nature nudged me to stop and take stock, right up to the moment when the snow slid. Tragically, I lacked the courage to listen to my best self.

Adventure's metaphors are worthy of trust because they illustrate universal truths about being human – not by telling, but by showing. I had experienced many adventure events in my life, but without stillness as a counterpoint, they never metabolized into anything that had meaning or use. In making sense of this tragedy, I have been gifted with the truth that every powerful event in my life of adventure includes an instructive metaphor with the power to transform my life in ways I could never have imagined.

METAPHOR'S TRUTH ABOUT BEING BURIED

Being buried felt commonplace, as if it were all familiar. Socially, I had spent most of my life under the surface of things. No one knew me, including myself. Being hidden felt easier because I was in my "protected cocoon." I had learned, somewhere along the way, that hiding myself reduced the pain of rejection. Convinced that being vulnerable was too much, I ambled though life like a ghost that was real and unreal at the same time. The agony of human relationships. The suffering of confrontation. The heartbreak of rejection. These were all things to which I was a slave because my fear of them, and my actions to avoid them, only increased their power in my life. Sadly my failure to build open relationships with myself and others was a path to pain anyhow.

The source of my striving to stay hidden is hard to know exactly, and likely unimportant. Childhood coping mechanisms might work for survival in crisis at that particular stage in life, but they are not something to be nurtured and maintained into adulthood. Understanding the source of my behaviour is not a solution, especially if it is identified in order to blame. I chose to isolate because I was not skilled enough to know that it was okay to feel pain and learn from it.

Being dug out by John, Age, Joe and Rick, slapped across the face and told to wake up was a powerful moment to live. I carry its meaning with me. Our true nature craves to be free from encumbrances and free to experience beauty when we soar. True freedom comes from being open, letting go of judgment, and waking. That slap, harsh as it might appear, was a deep act of compassion, an invitation to wake up to my true nature.

METAPHOR'S TRUTH ABOUT FALSE ALARMS

A false alarm has the potential to divert a responder's attention away from legitimate emergencies. My pulling that fire alarm as a boy could have taken resources away from a real emergency. My legitimate emergency was in not having good relationships where I could be authentic and transparent with myself and those around me. My emergency was isolation and how I responded to it. I never understood that. As a small boy, I could not comprehend that by pulling that alarm, I was calling for help not for a fire that didn't exist, but for a profoundly hazardous isolation that did. Once I'd grown to adulthood, this isolation grew into crisis because it shrouded my reasons for doing things, even from myself. Not knowing my reasons for my choices lowered my decision-making into unconsciousness. This was my normal. But being comfortable operating in this way is profoundly hazardous. I got used to feeling something inside and not addressing it in the real world because of a need for acceptance. I also got used to silencing the alarm bells that rang just before I made a poor choice.

I inhabited distortion rather than truth. On the morning of, and moments before, the avalanche, I treated accuracies being conveyed through my instincts as erroneous. But they were not. When making decisions that affect people's lives, this way of being is hazardous.

Being a mature human being comes from exercising discernment about what is real and what is illusion. By befriending fear and being honest about all aspects of what we experience, and working with individuals who can and do encourage the same, we can build a guidance system for life. Honesty and truth are critical in managing negative consequence in high-risk environments. Ruedi and I did not understand the power of truth. Therefore, we created tragic consequence.

METAPHOR'S TRUTH ABOUT ICE AND ICE CLIMBING

Ice is impermanent. It disappears in a couple of ways. It can melt and become water, or it can skip the liquid stage altogether and change from its solid form directly into a gas, through a process called sublimation. The transitory nature of ice has always been front and centre for me as an ice climber, but I never metabolized my knowledge of that transitoriness into an educative metaphor.

Everything about ice and ice climbing is like mandala sand paintings. The fleeting existence of mandala sand paintings mirrors the transitory nature of ice and ice climbing. In Buddhist tradition, a mandala is created out of coloured sand. For weeks, monks sit and carefully place coloured sand, grain by grain, to create the mandala image. When the sand painting is done, it is briefly enjoyed, then swept up and poured into the river. The reason? Understanding and accepting impermanence, cultivating the ability to let go of attachments, and directing attention to the energy that fuels the process, the thing that cannot be destroyed.

The ice climbs I have ascended are gone, never to be experienced again in the same way, by me or anyone else. The goals I worked so hard to achieve were rendered meaningless when others eclipsed them. I was blinded by the objectives I set for myself. Like the ice climber anchored to a frozen waterfall, I anchored my whole being to the impermanence of success. Getting to the top was everything to me, including getting to the top of La Traviata and Tumbledown. My single-mindedness toward an objective blinded me to consequence. In an instant, all of those goals I had anchored to were vaporized. The reality on which I'd based my being changed into something I foolishly had not anticipated.

After the avalanche my identity shattered. It had been predicated on the idea that I was a safe individual. That notion was gone. In the grip of profound failure and shame, I was rudderless. Stripped down to what seemed like nothing, my whole mental construct of my life crumbled. All the things I had spent a lifetime building got swept up in the tragedy and pain my actions had caused for so many. The only thing that remained, the only thing lasting, was my spirit. Something seemingly intangible like water vapour, but more real than anything else.

The goals I set for myself are important. But like the monk sitting down to create a mandala, it is critical to understand what is real and what is not. The journey of the spirit is the thing. Listening to spirit is the best guide.

METAPHORICAL TRUTH AT SISYPHUS SUMMITS

Sisyphus, rolling a rock uphill. Forever. This metaphor is profound for a climber, especially since there is no purpose assigned to the work of climbing. In this case, the name of the route centres on the idea that Sisyphus actually makes it to the top.

On that day Nancy and I climbed Sisyphus Summits, I was affected by a comment so profoundly that I foolishly gave my power away. I raced for the top, believing I was in control, but the situation owned me. Events outside of my being became my inner reality. However, inside each of us is a deeper voice of wisdom. In accessing that wisdom, we are no longer stuck to an eternity of rolling the rock uphill.

Recently I spoke about the avalanche to a group in a homeless shelter. If one wants to find wisdom, it is rarely in the halls of privilege. There at the shelter, I found that the people I spoke with knew what I was conveying on a deeper level. At the end of my talk one of the men said to me, "You are so lucky!" I was taken aback because that was not something I could possibly claim, given all the suffering the event had caused. "How so?" I asked. He replied, "You had a very clear rite of passage." The clarity of his statement helped me feel more deeply. For it was not the event itself that I needed, but the growth it asked me to embark upon that was instructive for me.

The assumption we often make in our Western society is that when we reach physical maturity we also reach psychological maturity. We do not. In Western traditions, we lack a clear point at which we leave the adolescent behind and adopt the behaviours of the adult. Robert Kegan, a Harvard psychologist who studies adult development, has identified that 58 per cent of adults in our society still operate, psychologically, as adolescents, a stage where the individual does as the group does and believes as they believe.

Heading up the slope of La Traviata, I was following. When confronted by a challenging attitude on Sisyphus Summits, I took the bait. Failing to step out from the crowd and fashion my own response to situations, I remained imprisoned in my adolescent reality, still rolling the rock uphill.

My escape, my summiting, was in choosing to grow from the events I lived. My escape from the prison of meaningless pursuits in the mountains came from making meaning. My rite of passage: taking responsibility for my actions.

Truth is everything. It is woven into the fabric of our lives. It speaks to us in a subtle voice, but it is there, like a wise elder who utters gems in whispers. It is up to us to lean in and capture what is being said.

Ruedi Beglinger claims there were no mistakes made. But this event has been so pain-filled for so many that it is desperately hard to believe this to be true. However, given how unconscious I was, I am not sure anything but a hard lesson would have gotten my attention. Therefore, it does not feel like a mistake that the consequences of our choices were so catastrophic. Tragedy stopped me so I could have a deep look at myself and learn to listen to the whispers. By listening deeply to everything, I can now navigate my life with less suffering.

CHAPTER 12

LESSON EIGHT: GRACE

The first printing of *Buried* drew me into an ongoing mentorship through the process of sharing the content of its pages with others. Five years after the release of the book I continue to learn from speaking to groups and answering their questions. Sharing my learning has deepened its lessons for me, and there is now a much greater sense of well-being in my life. Healing came from two places. First, from becoming accountable for my actions. Second, from forgiving myself.

Accountability has meant discovering the often very personal and uncomfortable reasons for my actions and sharing them in these pages. Standing in hard for those truths has been a rite of passage from one way of being in the world to another. Clearly, like most human experiences, I needed these lessons. Life itself is a mentor, and to have the humility to listen and learn from the small lessons helps mitigate the big painful ones.

Last year, 29-year-old Jiskarat Sidhu pleaded guilty

to 16 counts of dangerous driving causing death and 13 counts of dangerous driving causing bodily harm after failing to stop at a stop sign. Because of his actions at the time, the transport truck he was driving in the spring of 2018 crashed into a bus carrying the Humboldt Broncos hockey team. At the time of this writing his sentencing is pending. Sidhu's act of accountability has had an immediate and palpable effect of healing in the Humboldt, Saskatchewan, community. The relief on the faces of those who lost so much is visible even in their television interviews. Sidhu made a mistake, one that most of us who drive a car have made. Nonetheless he is accepting his punishment, which will likely be time in jail, because he broke a law and the consequence of his error affected so many. Sidhu has shown great maturity in claiming responsibility.

I understand now that if we had had the courage to do the same in the days and months after the disaster of La Traviata, almost everyone connected with that incident would be healthier and freer today. It took me far too long to become accountable for my actions on that day, and many suffered too long because of it.

Forgiving myself is still difficult some days. When I do, it comes from the understanding that given the situation and how I was being challenged, I was doing my best. As strange as it sounds, and as profoundly ridiculous as the events leading up to the tragedy were, I lacked the strength of awareness in those circumstances and at that moment to make the situation better. At the time, I believed my powerlessness made it safer. I no longer believe that.

Forgiveness also came from understanding that I have things to learn on this journey of life, and that I humbly continue to learn them. There is little I can do about that horrific tragedy to make it better except one thing: share with others the learning and teachings I have been granted.

On my journey of sharing, shortly after the first box of books was delivered, I travelled to Truckee, California, to engage with the community that lost Kathy Kessler (Polucha) in November 2014. Janice Polucha, Kathy's sister, hosted breakfast in her home in Nevada City the morning I arrived. It was a lovely gathering with her brother Bob and Heidi Biber, Kathy's best friend, who was with us on La Traviata and who performed CPR on many of the victims that day.

If there was a theme to that morning's conversations, it was grace. As a guest, I could have been received with anger and bitterness, but entering Janice's home was to become a step into grace. The table was set for a small lovely group gathered in peace and tranquility. I shared copies of the book and we talked without discomfort. Heidi and I connected after the dozen years that had passed, and shared our experiences of the event with the others. I came to better understand how deeply the tragedy, and the loss of Kathy, had affected everyone.

After breakfast Janice and I drove down to the Yuba river, a deep and beautiful granite-boulder river canyon that Janice visits to achieve her own personal grounding and healing. It is one of her sacred spaces, where she allows nature to inform and transform her life. The river was low after a few drought years, but emerald-green waters still flowed among the rounded granite rocks. We danced from stone to stone along the rocky shore until we came to a group of larger boulders. There we paused and Janice picked up a football-sized rock and balanced it lengthwise on the prominent edge of a large white boulder to represent her sister Kathy. We then chose more stones for Craig, Dennis, Naomi, Dave, Jean-Luc and Vern, setting them up in a balanced grouping, and as we did we were gifted by a palpable presence of the seven. I was surprised by the power of those stones on that ledge. Finding their balance points centred us as well; I found my own balance there among them. To mark my arrival, Janice had generously created a ceremony which would help me feel welcome and empowered for the task ahead.

After our river sojourn, I drove up to Truckee and got set up for my talk at The Bookshelf. In retrospect, I regretted not having reserved a better location. Not that the bookstore was a bad venue, but if I had fully understood the depth of what was about to happen, I would have, out of respect, preferred a proper theatre. I set up the projector to show its images on a bedsheet we had purchased from the second-hand store next door. We pushed bookshelves aside to have more room for chairs. When the time came for my presentation and reading, the room was filled beyond capacity with people both seated and standing. The whole community had came to listen to what I had to say about how Kathy lost her life. I should have been profoundly intimidated, but fortunately the morning's river ceremony had prepared me.

Gathered were Kathy's friends and family. Her 90-year-old mother, Madeline, her sister Annie, brother Bob, sister Janice, their niece Dawn, and of course Scott Kessler, Kathy's widower. Also in attendance were Peter Millar, Keith Lindsay, Rick Martin, Heidi Biber, Craig Dostie and a host of others extending all the way out onto the sidewalk, with the door left ajar so they wouldn't be shut out.

I spoke about the snowpack on that fateful day long ago, the lack of communication between myself and Ruedi, and the errors we had made with our aggressive approach to the conditions. I showed images of the slope that indicated the positions of our two groups, and read from the pages of my newly published book. After my reading about the avalanche and my experiences in it, Madeline, who had lost her daughter Kathy, said in a surprisingly supportive tone of voice, "This is so interesting." Her comment was completely disarming. Never before in my life had I witnessed such grace from someone who had lost so much.

The next evening I was invited to dinner by Scott Kessler and his partner, Kristin. They prepared a lovely meal in their beautiful home. We talked at length about all manner of subjects, including books we had read. Scott punctuated the conversation by saying, "Ken, I want to thank you for coming down here. We all waited a long time to hear the details about how Kathy died. I know ski touring is dangerous and I accept that. But knowing what happened brings a sense of closure to these events that many of us needed."

Reflecting on Scott's comment, I understand that I let fear win in the long days, weeks, months and years after the avalanche. All of that time added up to the 12 years the family of the victims had to wait to hear the details of what happened. Now I know I lost my humanity for all that time because I was scared. I had begun to lose it while on the slopes of La Traviata, and I lost a lot more of it afterward by adhering to the protocol of "not speaking to anyone" issued by the lawyer. I had been wrapped up in my own fear, and had no perspective beyond what was happening to me. Sitting down to dinner with Scott, and the grace he showed through expressing his gratitude, finally brought me to an acute awareness of and empathy with their suffering.

It was a long drive from Truckee, California, back to Vancouver Island, and the whole way home I began to understand that I was finally doing the right things.

EPILOGUE

It is often said that wanting things to be different than they are is the root of all suffering, and I've finally found this to be true. I have learned my lessons from La Traviata. I have passed these lessons on to my community, and with that I pass the responsibility and accountability for learning the human lessons from the La Traviata tragedy on to my guiding community.

On March 11, 2019, a guided group of women ice climbers went to a waterfall climb called Masseys, located at the base of a large avalanche slope with clear trim lines visible from the highway near Field, BC. At around 2 p.m., while the group was practising V thread anchors at the base of the climb, an avalanche came down and buried Michelle Klote and Sonja Johnson Findlater. All of the backpacks with probes and shovels were buried deep in snow at the base of the ice wall. Responders were rendered nearly powerless without probes and shovels available. Michelle's head was near the surface and was cleared away by a rescuer, so she was left trapped while the rescue effort continued for Sonia. The scene was horrific. Michelle, with one hand available, made several calls for help with her cell phone from her trapped position. Sonia was extricated and flown to hospital but later died of her injuries.

GLOSSARY

alpine touring: Or backcountry ski touring, is a method of ski mountaineering. Climbing uphill is possible with a binding that articulates and with skins on the skis for climbing. Descents are made possible by removing the climbing skins and locking down the boot heels to alpine ski down.

anchor: A fixed point in rock, ice or snow to which a climber or mountaineer secures. These can consist of various rock climbing hardware, ice screws or buried items in the snow.

belay: (verb) The action of mindfully being aware of a climber's progress and feeding a rope through a friction device or system to protect their progress. (noun) A stance or position that a climber uses to anchor to rock or ice before being able to protect a second climber.

bergschrund: A crevasse that forms the upper edge of dynamic glacier ice where it meets static alpine ice. Alpine ice is static because there is little accumulation of snow on the steep faces to compress, turn into ice and gain fluid volume through increased mass.

bolt: Pre-placed rock protection affixed by boring a hole into the rock with a power drill, hammering 3/8-inch-diameter, four-inch-long stainless steel stock into the hole and bolting a metal loop (hanger) onto it for clipping carabiners to. These bolts have an expansion mechanism which, when loaded with an outward pull, keeps them from popping out. When placed in good rock, a bolt can sustain up to 24 kN (kilonewtons) of force, or about 5,400 pounds.

cam: A three- or four-spring-loaded camming unit and compression trigger that is placed in parallel-sided rock cracks to protect the climber. These come in different sizes for cracks of various widths.

climbing skin: A synthetic "sealskin" with a non-permanent adhesive that sticks to the base of a ski, allowing the alpine tourer to ski uphill without sliding backward.

carabiner: An aluminum snap-link used to connect a climbing rope to anchor points placed in the rock, snow or ice.

col: A small pass between two peaks, typically with steep access on all sides.

convex roll: A convexity in a mountain slope, typically where the snow is most under tension.

cornice: An unmoving, overhanging wave of snow that forms through the action of wind on the leeward side of a slope or ridge.

couloir: A steep gully on a mountainside, typically filled with ice or snow.

crag: A rock cliff.

crevasse: A crack that forms in glacier ice that is in tension as it flows over a convexity in the bedrock beneath the ice. Crevasses become problematic when they are bridged with snow, because they are unseen and the bridge may not support the weight of a climber or skier. See also *glacier* below.

crown fracture: The fracture-line wall left at the top of a slope after a slab avalanche of snow has broken away and slid down.

free solo (solo): Climbing without the use of ropes or systems to protect the climber's progress.

glacier: A dynamic body of ice that forms through compaction and compression of snow over time. Glaciers reside in alpine or polar regions of the world where winter snows do not always completely melt in the summer; the ice is subject to the forces of gravity and therefore flows over the terrain and downvalley, much like a slow-moving river. See also *crevasse* above.

hanger: A stainless-steel loop that, in combination with a bolt, provides a secure point for climbers to clip into with their carabiners.

harness: A waist belt and corresponding leg loops worn by climbers or mountaineers to connect themselves to technical-mountaineering or rock- or ice-climbing systems.

haulbag: A smooth, cylindrical bag with straps on top for carrying food, water and equipment up rock or alpine faces.

headwall: The highest and steepest part of a slope or cliff.

jumar: A mechanical ascender for a climbing rope. Jumars are used for a person climbing a rope or in a mechanical-advantage system for ratcheting up loads.

moraine: Rock till that has been transported by the movement of glacier ice. It is characterized by stones of varying size, unlike till that has been transported by liquid water. Moraines may be termed lateral, medial or terminal, based on their position relative to the flowing glacier.

pass: Route through mountains, typically between two peaks.

pitch: A stretch of climbing on ice or rock determined by rope length, climb features or limitations of belay stances or protection.

probe (avalanche): An aluminum pole used for probing snow depth, for finding snow-bridged crevasses on a glacier, for staying solidly on a mountain ridge and not wandering out onto a cornice, and for confirming the location of an avalanche victim buried under the snow after a transceiver search is completed or through the long process of a probe line search.

quickdraw: A short sling with two carabiners used to attach a rope to fixed points in rock, snow or ice to protect a climber.

radio: very high frequency (VHF) radio for use for communication in the mountains. Communication is line of sight, so repeaters are placed high on mountaintops to relay messages and enable greater range.

rillenkarren: Solution fluting in limestone that forms sharp vertical edges in the stone, caused by rainwater flowing down the face.

rock shoe: A tight-fitting, sticky, rubber-soled shoe used to provide greater adhesion to small rock edges while rock climbing.

rope: A climbing rope made of nylon that has dynamic qualities serving to lessen the energy of a climber's fall.

scree: A mass of fist-sized or smaller stones, typically accumulating below a cliff that is the source of the debris over time.

sérac: An ice cliff which forms when glacier ice flows off a high rock cliff. Typically séracs are a hazardous place to venture under, because of the unpredictability of large chunks of ice breaking off and falling.

slab: A cohesive unit of snow that bonds together through the action of wind or compaction over time.

talus: Fist-sized or larger rocks accumulated on a large mountain slope or field.

transceiver (avalanche): A device worn while travelling in avalanche terrain that can send and receive a radio signal at 457 kHz. The technology assists rescuers in locating individuals buried under snow by homing in on their signal to within 30 centimetres.

treeline: The margin of a landscape that has a long enough season and sufficient moisture to support tree growth. This line may be below alpine regions or above desert regions.

whumph: A technical term used to describe the resulting percussive sound when millions of snow grains shift during acute settling of a snowpack.

yo-yo ski: Using a single slope to do several runs, primarily for the experience of skiing or riding down in powder snow.

REFERENCES

1. Environment Canada, "Daily Data Report for January 2003: Glacier NP Mt Fidelity, BC." HTML downloadable as CSV spreadsheet. Accessed Aug. 15, 2014, at http://is.gd/SR3wbU.

2. Larry Stanier, "Coroner's Report from the Avalanche Accident on La Traviata, Durrand Glacier Area, Northern Selkirks, January 20, 2003." (Avalanche consultant report to BC coroner, March 2003): 3.

3. Frank Baumann, "Analysis of the Durrand Glacier Avalanche Accident, January 20, 2003," a private investigation for Peter Millar and Annie Polucha Millar. Squamish, BC: Baumann Engineering, March 15, 2004. Accessed August 15, 2014 (pdf) at http://webpages.charter.net/pmillar/Durrand%20Report.pdf.

4. Stanier, 3.

5. British Columbia Coroner's Report, RCMP Statement, "Severed Statement," Ken Wylie, January 20, 2002, Revelstoke, BC.

6. Oscar Wilde, quoted at *Good Reads*. Accessed Aug. 15, 2014, at www.goodreads.com/quotes/329316-with-age-comes-wisdom-but-sometimes-age-comes-alone.

7. "Steve Podborski looks back at 'Crazy Canucks' years." CBC Digital Archives, broadcast Jan. 2, 2007, 19:12. Streaming video accessed Aug. 15, 2014, www.cbc.ca/player/Sports/Digital+Archives/Skiing/ID/1739493212/.

8. "The 'Crazy Canucks' more famous in Europe." CBC Digital Archives, broadcast Mar. 6, 1979, 9:54. Streaming video accessed Aug. 15, 2014, at www.cbc.ca/player/Digital+Archives/ID/1438858030/.

9. "Brené Brown: The Power of Vulnerability." TEDxHouston, filmed June 2010, 20:19. Streaming video accessed Aug. 15, 2014, at www.ted.com/talks/brene_brown_on_vulnerability.

10. Stephen R. Covey, *The 7 Habits of Highly Effective People: Powerful Lessons in Personal Change*, New York: Simon and Schuster, 1989.

KEN WYLIE is an internationally certified mountain guide and a member of the International Federation of Mountain Guides Associations, the Association of Canadian Mountain Guides and the American Mountain Guides Association. Originally from Alberta, Canada, he has led expeditions worldwide, in Canada, New Zealand and Peru as well as to Denali and Joshua Tree. Ken's 30 years of experience as a mountain guide and experiential educator includes work for such organizations as Yamnuska Mountain School, Outward Bound Canada and Outward Bound USA. Ken founded Mountains for Growth in 2013 to help individuals and groups gain personal insight and wisdom through outdoor adventures.